NO
WITNESSES

NO WITNESSES

The story of Robbery and Murder at the
Cabinet Supreme Savings and Loan

KATE MARCH
WITH HOWARD MAKIN

Library of Congress Control Number: 2007910026
ISBN: Hardcover   978-1-4363-1030-7
                 Softcover   978-1-4363-1029-1

To order additional copies of this book, contact:
Xlibris Corporation
1-888-795-4274
www.Xlibris.com
Orders@Xlibris.com
43113

Contents

DEDICATION

To my husband, Pat, and my son, Alan,
whose active and moral support made this book possible.

Foreword

The Cabinet Supreme murders shocked Delhi Township and the entire Greater Cincinnati area. The story was covered extensively at the time, and is rehashed when the murderers come up for parole. However, the complete story has never been told, until now.

Kate March covered the story in 1969 as editor of the *Price Hill News* (now the *Price Hill Press*). More than twenty-five years later, she completed the manuscript for this book. Her research included interviews with the key characters in the case, including many hours in prison interviewing convicted murderer John Leigh. The trial transcripts, investigation notes, and personal reminiscences of those involved have all been pulled together in this book, to tell the tale of petty thugs out of control, resulting in mass murder. This book tells the story of excellent police work, cooperation between police agencies, the lifestyle of the petty criminals who became murderers, and life in the Ohio prison system. The impact of the murders on the lives of the victim's families is not forgotten.

This private printing of *No Witnesses* allows the story to finally be told to all.

Alan March, Cincinnati, Ohio
January 2008

At the time of the murders and robbery, the Cabinet Supreme crime was the most heinous to ever occur in Hamilton County, Ohio, and its tri-state environs. It probably exists as such yet today. The shock created in this community by this senseless crime was horrific. Just as those who were alive at the time of the assassination of President Kennedy recall what they were doing when they heard of the president's death, those who were alive at the time of the Cabinet Supreme murders and robbery remember what they were doing when they learned of the crime.

The array of multi-jurisdictional law enforcement put together at my disposal, in a matter of minutes, had never been accomplished before. Due to the success of this case, it has been done many times since. It always seems to prevail.

As the book defines, so many people contributed to the successful conclusion of this case. This was remarkable. The amount of evidence the crime-scene and identification technicians were able to come up with was nothing short of amazing. The witnesses and other information gathered by hard working police officers, doing what they do best, was equally important to the successful conclusion of this case. With all that, the fact is, the case was aided most by good old fashioned police work performed by Delhi officers Eschenbach and Jasper *prior* to the murders.

This book portrays a behind the scenes look at some of the obstacles encountered in most major crime case investigations. It also portrays the good, the bad, and the ugly that existed in our society then and even more so today.

I miss my dear friend Kate March. I'm grateful to her for pushing and cajoling me into joining her in this endeavor and letting her do her thing in telling this story. I miss you Kate!

Howard Makin, 2008

Howard Makin died May 3, 2008, just months after writing these lines. He was 78 years old.

Acknowledgments

Tracing the twenty-five year story of the aftermath of multiple murder involved a lot of people whose assistance is greatly appreciated. Some preferred not to be named, and in those instances, an asterisk in the text will indicate that a pseudonym has been used. Among others whose help has been of great value to this work are Walter Rischmann and family; Rosemary Stitzel; Thomas Stahlheber, Delhi Township zoning administrator; the staff of the Hamilton County Clerk of Courts with one notable exception; Tom Callabro of the Hamilton County Board of Elections; Mark Adkins, prosecutor's investigator in Greene County, Ohio; my nephew, Albert Novick; the historical desk at the Lima, Ohio, public library; Joe Andrews of the Ohio Department of Rehabilitation and Correction; and most of all, the good people of the Delhi Township Police Department.

Kate March, Beavercreek, Ohio
August, 1995

Chapter One

The Holdup

7:00 am, Wednesday, September 24

John Leigh and his friend, Graham Davis, got up early despite having been out drinking most of the night at the 226 Club, one of Cincinnati's first gay bars. It was a favorite haunt for the men, who had met there about two years ago when Leigh, better known as Johnny, was cruising, looking for a buck.

They hadn't gotten to bed until three that morning, but Davis had to be at work by 8:00 a.m. Leigh had no job, but he got up, too, because he knew if he drove Davis to work, he could use his friend's Chevy Malibu convertible for the rest of the day. Johnny told Graham he needed it to take his wife to the bus station. It was a lie.

Johnny felt Godawful, all that booze and very little sleep. He felt as if alcohol saturated his entire one-hundred-and-fifty pound body and was seeping out his pores. But he was hell-bent on the day's agenda. He stared bleary-eyed into the bathroom mirror as he fingered the wispy Vandyke beard he had carefully cultivated. A slender five feet eight at age twenty, Leigh grew the beard because he got tired of being called a kid.

He splashed some water on his face, ran a comb quickly through his unruly mop of hair, then gave up.

The two men went out to the convertible and Leigh got behind the wheel. He dropped his friend off at the University of Cincinnati Medical Center print shop, where Davis had been employed for about ten years, then drove down the hill to Race Street to meet Red Johnson.

Leigh and Johnson first met at a buddy's house just a few weeks earlier. Since then, they shot pool together a few times at Art's Pool Hall on upper Vine Street, but today was going to be different. Today they were going to make some serious money.

The two were an unlikely pair. Red was big, six feet three and heavyset, with bright red kinky hair. He was as quiet as his smaller companion was talkative. Johnson was only two years older than Leigh, but the quiet giant was an imposing presence. People did not forget him.

Leigh picked up Johnson at his home, then drove to his own Wheeler Street apartment to tell his wife he was okay, that he would be home again about noon. Rita, still in bed and not quite awake, just nodded. She wasn't surprised. Johnny had stayed out all night before. Nor was she surprised at the big, quiet red-haired guy who was with her husband, a man who just stood there and said nothing. Her Johnny knew some strange people. Rita went back to sleep and the two men went back to their car.

They headed for the Sixth Street viaduct, where twenty-four-year-old Ray Kassow waited.

8:15 am, Wednesday

Kassow was sitting in his old Ford Falcon on English Street, a short, insignificant byway lying shadowed under the viaduct. There was neither residence nor business along the darkened street. People meeting there didn't attract much attention. Leigh pulled over, parked behind the Falcon, and all three men got out of their cars.

Kassow went to the trunk of his car and took out a laundry bag and a burlap bag, handling them carefully. He placed them on the hood of the Malibu convertible just behind him. He reached into the two bags and withdrew three guns, placing them on top of the bags on the car hood. The other two watched paunchy, half-bald Kassow as he methodically loaded two .22 caliber revolvers, one of them newly stolen, wiping every bullet with a handkerchief before it went into the chamber.

"What are you doing that for, Ray?" Leigh asked.

"No fingerprints. You know," Kassow said. Leigh didn't know. It didn't make a lot of sense to him, wiping bullets, but he shrugged and shut up. What the hell, it was Ray's plan.

As he loaded each revolver, Kassow handed it to Leigh, saying, "Here. Put it on the front seat of my car." But he didn't hand over the automatic. He hefted it, staring at the weapon. A sixth grade drop-out, Kassow didn't know much, but he knew guns, and this one bothered him. He glanced up at a streetlight, took aim and fired.

"Damn, Ray! What are you doing?" Leigh was startled. "Somebody's gonna hear that!"

"Nah," Kassow replied. "They'll just think it's a car backfiring." Traffic zoomed along the busy viaduct overhead, and nearby was heavily traveled River Road. "This gun jams sometimes. I'm just testing." He fired again. Exasperated and hyped up, Leigh looked at Johnson who just stared and said nothing. But Kassow stopped shooting. He put a fresh magazine in the automatic, got into his Ford and put the gun with the others.

"Okay, now you guys follow me." Kassow drove around the block to Storrs Street, followed by the other two in the Chevy convertible. Kassow parked his car on Storrs, picked up the guns and got into the front passenger seat of the convertible. Johnson sat quietly in the rear.

With Leigh at the wheel of the borrowed car, they drove west on River Road, headed for Delhi Township.

*   *   *

Five miles down the road, they turned right, driving up steeply winding Anderson Ferry Road, and ended in the Kroger parking lot next to their target, the Cabinet Supreme Savings and Loan on Delhi Pike.

"Now," said Kassow, "we just set and wait."

"Wait for what?" Leigh wanted to know. He was feeling lousy and wanted to get it on.

"Well, see, the man inside—the manager, I think—he goes out every morning, and then there'll be only one person inside, the teller."

It was a long wait. Leigh got out of the car and went into Frisch's, a neighboring restaurant, where he picked up a carry out order of two coffees for himself and Kassow, and a large lemonade for Johnson. The waitress would later remember him as a man who made the unusual purchase of lemonade during the breakfast rush.

While Leigh was in the restaurant, Ray Kassow got out of the car and moved into the driver's seat. He was spotted by a man who knew him and disliked him. The man also had seen Kassow's face on the Delhi Police bulletin board, and wondered why Kassow was in a town where the police were interested in him. On impulse, the man jotted down the license plate number of the convertible.

Leigh came back to the car and the three men killed some time drinking. Kassow decided it was time to distribute the guns. He handed the automatic to

Leigh, now in the passenger seat, turned to the back and gave a white-handled revolver to Johnson. The revolver with the black grip he placed on the console between the two bucket seats in the front of the car. And the men waited.

*   *   *

Henrietta and Luella Stitzel were getting ready to go out. Both in their sixties, the women were very close, more like sisters than sisters-in-law. They had married brothers who as children had emigrated with their parents from Germany to Cincinnati. The boys' parents prospered in their new country and purchased a house on Denver Street in Lower Price Hill. Now the parents were long gone and the house was shared by Luella and her husband, Nicholas Stitzel, and by Henrietta and her six children.

Nick's brother, Matthew, died in 1953 at age 51, leaving Henrietta with five daughters and two sons. One son would follow his father to the graveyard nine years later, the result of an industrial accident. When Matthew was taken on his last journey to the hospital, he extracted a promise from his brother to take care of the children. Nick promised freely to do so. He and Luella were childless, and they both loved his brother's children.

Henrietta's eldest daughter, Rosemary, thinks fondly of her Uncle Nick. "He was always there for his girls, as he called us," said Rosemary. It was Rosemary's twin, Robert, who died in the industrial accident at age twenty-two.

Nick was a caring, surrogate father to Henrietta's children, and Luella was like a second mother. When Henrietta was busy with the younger children, her sister-in-law frequently took the older children downstairs for tea, toast and talk with Aunt Luella. She also took them shopping, or swimming, to the zoo and to visit Santa at Christmas. Some expeditions included neighborhood kids, who also called the Stitzels Aunt Luella and Uncle Nick.

As the children grew older, Henrietta and Luella became even closer. They did everything together, going to mass at Blessed Sacrament Church on Wilder Avenue and attending meetings of the Married Ladies Sodality. They made joint forays to their favorite bakery and did banking errands, such as they planned this Wednesday.

Dressed for an outing, both women wore blue, although Luella's dress was checkered while Henrietta's was striped. Each woman wore a black cloth coat and white leather shoes. They were much alike.

Henrietta gathered the family's seven Christmas Club books; two were her own, two belonged to her daughter, Rosemary, and one each belonged to daughters Margaret, Ann, and Marilyn. From habit, she carried with her the latest issue of *Maryknoll Magazine*. The women got into Nick's car and headed for Cabinet Supreme Savings and Loan in Delhi Township.

10:45 am, Wednesday

The three men sitting in the Chevy convertible in Delhi were getting edgy with the wait. Finally, Manager Jerry Grueter emerged from the savings and loan, got into his station wagon, and drove west on Delhi Pike, then south down Anderson Ferry Road. The trio in the waiting vehicle followed him halfway down Anderson Ferry Road, making sure he wasn't just driving around the block. But Grueter continued on. He had an appointment on nearby Hillside Avenue.

"Okay, I guess he's gonna be gone for a while," Kassow said. He turned the convertible around, heading back up the hill to the savings and loan where he pulled into the small lot and backed up against the building to park. The only other car in the lot belonged to the teller.

*   *   *

Kassow stayed behind the wheel while Leigh and Johnson started to get out of the car. Kassow stopped them, saying, "Now there's only one person in there, the teller. And we can't have any witnesses, you understand? No witnesses. If anyone else goes in behind you, I'll follow them and kill them."

Testily, Leigh responded, "Okay, okay." Leigh and Johnson got out of the car and went into the building. It was a couple of minutes before 11 a.m.

11:00 am, Wednesday

Helen Huebner usually cashed her paycheck at a bank near McAlpin's Department Store downtown where she was a part-time sales clerk. But today her husband, Joe, picked her up after leaving his job at the Wiedemann Brewery across the Ohio River in Newport, Kentucky. She decided to cash her check at Cabinet Supreme on the way to their Delhi Township home. They had had an account there for eight years.

Joe and Helen, married for twenty-three years, worked hard to support their three boys. They were looking forward to seeing their oldest, Tom, who was nearing the end of his tour of duty with the U.S. Navy and would soon be home. Still at home were his younger brothers, Daniel, who attended Our Lady of Victory Elementary School, and Larry, a student at Oak Hills High School.

The Huebner parents got to Cabinet Supreme about eleven in the morning. Joe drove into the little lot next to the savings and loan and parked to the right of the lot. He usually parked on the left side, but there were already three cars there, and the parking area was small. Joe recognized one of the cars. It belonged to the teller. He saw two women in another car who had driven in just ahead of him. The third car was a dirty old Chevrolet convertible, parked right behind him.

Joe parked facing east, away from the building. In his rearview mirror, he could see the walk in front of the doorway and the convertible.

Sitting next to him, Helen clutched her big red plastic purse, got out of the car, and headed for the door. Joe noticed the other two women walking toward the front door about the same time. He knew they all would get prompt service from the popular teller, Lillian Dewald, who had been with Cabinet Supreme Savings and Loan for thirteen years. Lillian was pleasant and efficient. A good-looker, too, a little over average height, weight all in the right places.

As the three women went into the building, Joe turned on the car radio, settled back and listened to music. He kept an eye on the mirror so he could spot Helen when she came out.

*   *   *

When Leigh and Johnson walked into the small thrift, Johnson went up to Lillian Dewald at the counter and said, "I want to make a deposit in my account." She was not particularly happy to see the big red-haired man again. He had been in before and acted strangely, Lillian thought. But she turned to pick up deposit slips. At that point, Leigh whipped out his automatic and Johnson announced, "This is a stick-up." Johnson reached into his back pocket, pulled out his white-handled revolver and pointed it at Lillian.

The teller stepped back, her eyes on the gun. Johnson reached over the counter and rifled the cash drawer, knocking to the floor a cardboard box holding account cards and deposit slips. As he grabbed a handful of money, three women walked through the front door. Leigh stared at them. "Oh shit!" Johnson turned his head, saw them, then looked back at Lillian behind the counter.

The newcomers walked just a few steps into the lobby, then stopped. Transfixed, they stared at the gun in Leigh's hand. For a moment, nobody moved. This was more than the holdup men had bargained for. It was a small office, and Kassow had said there was seldom more than a single customer at a time in the place, especially in the morning.

"Okay! Everybody into the vault!" Neither man later remembered who actually said the words. It all happened so fast.

Johnson took their handbags, and the four frightened women were herded into the six by ten foot vault, made more narrow by a safe and storage cabinets which lined the walls. The teller tried to duck between the safe and a filing cabinet, but the space was small and she still was exposed to the gunmen.

Johnny Leigh panicked. Hungover and unnerved by the unexpected presence of three more women, Kassow's *no witnesses* kept running through his head like a broken record. *No witnessess!* From the doorway of the vault, he faced the women—shaking from alcohol, little sleep and an adrenaline rush—and the gun went off.

Johnson stood stock still. At the sound of the first shot he turned to stone, a statue holding three women's pocketbooks and a .22 revolver.

Leigh kept shooting. One shot each felled the two older women who seemed to cling together. Then Helen Huebner dropped, a bullet in her head and her McAlpin's paycheck still in her left hand. The women fell on top of each other. There was no place else to fall.

Leigh fired twice at Dewald because she just kept screaming, then his gun jammed. He turned, snatched Johnson's gun out of his hand and fired again. Dewald fell forward, her head landing on the vault doorsill. Leigh stood over her, firing one more time. Then that gun jammed, but Lillian's screams had stopped.

A wispy thought found its way into Leigh's booze-soaked brain. This was all wrong. He shouted to Johnson, "Let's go!" but the big man didn't move.

"Christ, Red, come on!" Leigh finally took Johnson by the hand and led him out. They walked rapidly back to the convertible, where Kassow was watching and waiting.

Leigh and Johnson got into the car, and Kassow said excitedly, "I know two of those women! They're sisters, two of them who went in there. They live on my street! Are they all dead?"

Leigh snapped, "I guess so. Get the hell out of here." Kassow gunned the car and it took off, back the way they came.

Speeding east on the road along the Ohio River, Kassow gripped the wheel and stared straight ahead, his mind churning. Four women. All dead? "Did you really kill all those women?" He kept his eyes on the road, not looking at Red sitting next to him, or at Johnny in the back seat. Kassow didn't really believe anyone would actually be killed, despite his exhortations.

Leigh answered, "I think maybe one of them was still alive when we left."

Johnson broke his silence. "You had to do it," he said. John Leigh looked at the strange expression on Kassow's face and knew that what he had to do was get out of town.

*　　*　　*

Four women were murdered and they had missed their prime target, which was not the handful of bills from the cash drawer. John Leigh already had 400 stolen dollars in his pocket. Kassow wasn't carrying cash, but he had a $600 savings account of his own in a Cincinnati bank. What they went into the savings and loan to steal was "thousands of dollars of Jerry Grueter's own money" which Kassow had said the manager kept in a box in the vault. Kassow knew that in addition to Grueter's salary as manager of the savings and loan, he derived personal income from more than a dozen rental properties in the Eighth and State area. Kassow thought Grueter was rich, ripe for the plucking.

The unexpected arrival of the three women and quick shootings froze Johnson to immobility, and left Leigh with one thought: get away and get lost. Once the shooting started, the men didn't look for more money, never even tried to get at the safe or anything else. It was an ill-planned, almost ad lib hold-up.

* * *

Only minutes after Joe Huebner turned on his car radio, he glanced at his rearview mirror and sat bolt upright. He saw two men coming from the building at what he thought was a pretty fast gait. And one of them was carrying—it was unmistakable—his wife's big red purse. He watched them hurry along the walk towards the old Chevrolet convertible parked just behind his own car. Joe turned around to get a better look and watched them get into the Chevy. He could see a third man in the convertible. Joe jumped out of his own car and strained to read the license plate on the convertible as it pulled away, heading west on Delhi Pike.

Joe ran inside the building. There was no one in the lobby. He started walking towards the back, then was stopped in his tracks.

On the floor in a growing pool of blood, just beyond the swinging gate which separated the lobby from the office area, Joe Huebner saw Lillian Dewald. Her face was turned towards him, blood flowing from her nose and mouth. She was lying across the threshold of the small vault to the left of the office area.

Joe went to the vault door just in time to hear Lillian's last moan.

Behind Lillian in the narrow vault were three more women, grotesquely sprawled one on top of another in a bloody mess on the floor of the small walk-in vault. One of them was Helen, Joe's wife.

Huebner yelled, "Helen, are you hurt?" No answer. He screamed, "Helen, are you hurt?" Her head turned slightly, but she said nothing. It was the last move she ever made. The whole thing had happened so fast that Joe reached the vault as the last two women to be shot were taking their final breaths.

The horrified husband wanted to go to his wife, but hesitated about going into the vault. There wasn't room to move between the bodies and Helen was at the rear of the vault, toppled backwards across the head and shoulders of another woman. It was a deterring sight. Joe was reluctant to touch anything. Rather than handle the telephone in the savings and loan, he ran to the house next door to call for help.

11:12 am, Wednesday

Delhi Police Chief Howard Makin was in his office with two of his men. It was a routine planning session, suddenly shattered by a booming broadcast from the office monitor.

"Delhi Police Car number 829!" came the urgent voice of county communications. "Respond to Cabinet Supreme Savings and Loan on Delhi Pike. Armed robbery reported." The same imperative sent a county sheriff's patrol car to the scene.

Officer John Eschenbach, in the office with Makin, was running Car 829 that day. He bolted out of the room, picking up Officer Don Redman as he ran. Redman had just gone off-duty; he went anyway. They leaped into the cruiser and sped out of the Neeb Road police station.

Right behind them in a second cruiser was Chief Makin with another off-duty officer, Don Jasper, who had been part of the interrupted office talk. The cruiser radio crackled, "Vehicle seen leaving Cabinet Supreme is a 1953 or 1954 dark green Chevrolet bearing license plate 5344 BC." Makin saw Eschenbach head south on Neeb towards Delhi Pike, and told Jasper, at the wheel, to turn east on Rapid Run Pike.

Makin said, "If John and Don don't get them, they could head north on Anderson Ferry and maybe we can catch them at Anderson Ferry and Rapid Run." But the car they were hoping to see already had run in the other direction, south on Anderson Ferry Road towards River Road. As their cruiser raced the clock, Makin and Jasper heard another broadcast, for the Delhi Life Squad.

Four persons had been shot. The quiet suburban community was jarred to its rural roots.

*   *   *

Delhi Hills, christened Delhigh when it was established as a township in 1816, is ten-and-a-half square miles of rolling, hilly terrain above the Ohio River, just west of Cincinnati, Ohio. Some of it had been farmland, but primary occupations of early settlers kept the area in pasturage and greenhouses. Except for residential growth and a rising political consciousness, not much had changed by 1969. There weren't many cows and horses left, but many greenhouses still dotted the township which had grown to a population of 25,668.

It was a time of burgeoning suburbia, a place where people moved to get away from the city, to raise children in a less stressful environment. Slow and steady still characterized this suburban township, partially because of limited developable land. The 1990 census showed population growth of just 4,582 persons in the previous twenty years. Most of the greenhouses gave way to new home construction.

There had been considerable development along the major artery where Cabinet Supreme Savings and Loan had relocated from Lower Price Hill, but not much zoning change. The highly charged emotional zoning battles which characterize growth in many bedroom suburbs of large urban areas flared only briefly in Delhi. There was a transition period in the 1970s when the township threw off the yoke of county domination and established control of its own zoning destiny. The added commerce mostly has been within existing commercial corridors. Now, where there used to be blocks of homes interspersed with business along Delhi Pike, the private residence on that street is a rarity.

The little building which housed Cabinet Supreme still stood at the time of this writing, but it changed hands many times after the crime which no one living there has forgotten.

Chapter Two

Before the Fact

Before the holdup at Cabinet Supreme, Ray Kassow and Red Johnson did everything to call attention to themselves except stand under a flashing neon sign with an arrow pointing down at them, shouting, "Look at us!"

12:30 pm, Saturday July 12

Officer John Eschenbach of the Delhi Police answered the phone. It was Lou Lutz, owner of the Delhi Pike greenhouse operation which he called Tropical Foliage Plants. Lou was upset about two men who had just left his shop. He believed a check for $564.85 left with them.

Eschenbach drove around to the shop where Lutz told him, "My wife I and were back in the greenhouse and we heard these noises coming from my office. It sounded like the chair was scraping across the floor, like somebody was pulling it away from the desk. Then we could hear the desk drawer. It makes a little squeaky noise when it's pulled out. We both heard it. So I went in there and here were these two men standing at my desk."

Lutz demanded to know what they were doing in his office, and they said they just came in to get a couple of plants. "One of the guys bought two fifty-cent plants and then they both left, but I saw their car, an old Ford, and got the license number," Lutz told the officer.

"After I got the tag number, I went back and checked out the desk drawer and a check was missing," Lutz said. "It was made out to me for $564.85 from Sherman Floral in Cincinnati. That check was in that drawer, in an envelope, before," Lutz said.

It was not the first time these men had been in his shop, Lutz told Eschenbach, although it was the first time they came in together. "Once before, the big, redheaded guy came in and asked for shrubs," Lutz said. "I told him we don't handle shrubs, but he hung around for maybe five or ten minutes after that. Same thing happened with the other guy, one time."

Eschenbach checked out the license plate number which Lutz had picked up. It was registered to a 1961 two-door Ford under the name of Raymond Kassow of 1326 Denver Street. The address was in Lower Price Hill.

That was at the bottom of Cincinnati's Western Hills area. It was west of the four viaducts which span the Mill Creek and which separate east and west sides of the Queen City of the West physically, philosophically and in matters of heritage and custom.

East of the viaducts, residents predominantly were post-nineteenth century in their thinking and made a point of it. They read the *New York Times* and the *Washington Post*, preened themselves on an *au courant* attitude and were conspicuous spenders. On the westside, people tucked it away. Western Hills residents mostly were descendants of Cincinnati's early German settlers, with great pride in their conservative heritage. During the economic difficulties of the thirties and into the feisty forties, the Western Hills area developed a reputation as having more savings and loans than any similar size community in the country. The old virtues of family, faith and fiscal prudence were intact. Many still subscribed to the locally published German language newspaper.

Tradition was that as your economics improved, you moved up the hill from Lower Price Hill to Price Hill proper and Covedale, to Westwood and the general Western Hills area, even further west of which was Delhi Township. Lower Price Hill was at the bottom of the Western Hills economic scale.

Officer Eschenbach contacted Cincinnati Police District Three which covers the Price Hill area, both up and down the hills. Detective Frank Sefton in that district told him that he knew Raymond Kassow. He had questioned him in connection with a previous burglary charge.

Eschenbach and Sefton went together to Kassow's Denver Street home. There in the driveway was the car which had been described by the Delhi florist. A tall, red-haired man standing in the front yard next to the car identified himself as a Kassow friend, Watterson Johnson, of 1706 Race Street. That address was in the Over-the-Rhine area of the old German city.

"The Rhine" was the old Miami Canal, which met the Erie Canal at Dayton, Ohio and wound its way southwards to the Ohio River. The nickname derived from the large German immigrant population just north of the canal in Cincinnati. By the middle of the twentieth century, the old canal was paved over to become Central Parkway, and the character of the region changed, but the soubriquet stuck. One former resident described it as a slum.

"They call it Over-the-Rhine, but they didn't like what we called it," the man said. It was like a bad section of New York, so we called it the Rotten Apple." He referred to his home town as "Cincinnasty."

Both Kassow and Johnson freely admitted to police they had been at the Lutz floral shop where Kassow said he bought a couple of plants. They steadfastly denied taking the missing check.

Eschenbach reported that neither Kassow nor Johnson was employed. The officer said, "I think they took the envelope thinking it was cash and when they found out different, they destroyed the check." The check never did surface. No further action was possible.

4:30 am Sunday August 3

Officer Eschenbach, on patrol in the wee hours of the morning, spotted the Kassow car with Kassow and Johnson both in it, in the vicinity of Delfair Shopping Center on Delhi Pike. They were across the street from Cabinet Supreme Savings and Loan.

The cruising cop followed the Kassow car to Greenwell Avenue at Foley Road, where he stopped it. Eschenbach spoke to the two men and noticed a large amount of clothing in the back seat. There was more in the trunk. Kassow explained they were looking for a Goodwill box to deposit the clothes.

It was an odd hour to be looking for a Goodwill drop box. The story was additionally curious since they passed up two Goodwill boxes while the officer followed them. "I think they were taking from instead of putting in," Eschenbach said.

The men were allowed to go on, but Eschenbach wrote up a field interrogation report (FIR) on which he noted, again, both men were unemployed. The FIR was posted for the benefit of the next shift on the board at the police station, where it was noticed and remembered by a casual visitor to the station house.

12:45 pm, Thursday August 28

Delhi Officer Don Jasper was called to the Cabinet Supreme Savings and Loan at 5162 Delhi Pike. The teller, Mrs. Lillian Dewald, wanted to talk to police about two men who were in her office that morning. There was something about the way they looked, the way they acted, that raised her hackles.

She told Jasper, "I've worked here for thirteen years and this is the first time I've ever been afraid."

When the two men came in, one just stood looking around, mostly from behind a planter on the teller's counter. The other man told Mrs. Dewald he wanted to open an account with ten dollars. She gave him the necessary paperwork. When he returned the forms, she noticed he had omitted his social security number. She asked for it and the man sidled off, searching through his wallet. He finally gave her a number.

She asked him for the postal zone number of his address which was in the Over-the-Rhine area of Cincinnati. The man hesitated, then asked his companion what the zone number was. They came up with a number which Lillian did not believe was right. Besides, she told the Delhi officer, she was suspicious of anyone from Over-the-Rhine coming out to suburban Delhi to open a small savings account. It didn't make sense to her.

She also was worried because she was alone in the building. Manager Jerry Grueter was on vacation. They were, customarily, the only two persons in the office.

As Lillian Dewald sat at her desk, typing up the paperwork, she told the officer, she was convinced that when she got up from her typewriter and went back to the counter, one of them was going to put a gun in her face and hold her up. The premonition was prophetic.

But the man who opened the account as Watterson Johnson just gave her the ten dollars. She watched as the two of them left the building. They got into an old car, sat for a while, then drove off.

Descriptions given by the teller matched descriptions of Raymond Kassow and Watterson Johnson. Kassow was six feet tall and pudgy, with a deeply receding hairline and bushy eyebrows. Johnson stood six feet three inches, topped off with a head of hair that looked like a flaming Afro. One of his cheekbones was slightly higher than the other, producing a somewhat lopsided effect. They were hard to forget.

As soon as they left, Lillian called her husband, Walter Dewald, a Cincinnati traffic cop. He told her to call the Delhi Police Department. After speaking with the teller, Officer Jasper contacted the Cincinnati Police district which covered Over-the-Rhine and was told the address given was a vacant lot. Walter later did a personal drive-by of the address and saw it was not a vacant lot. The report was an error. There was a church on the ground floor with two apartments above it. He concluded it was possible that somebody lived there, that the address could be legitimate.

Jasper ran a computer check on Johnson, and came up blank. But a hand-check of Cincinnati records revealed an extensive juvenile record, starting with petty larceny when Watterson Johnson was only eleven years old. There followed charges of a burglary at age twelve; three burglaries at age thirteen and a burglary at age fourteen. Then he was sent to Boys' Industrial School (BIS) from which he escaped in May 1964 at the ripe old age of fifteen years. It was an established pattern of burglary. And police already knew Kassow as a man who had been convicted of one burglary and questioned about others.

As a precaution, Jasper asked Delhi Officer Robert Chetwood to report in plain clothes and stay inside the Cabinet Supreme building until closing time that day. Walter Dewald told Jasper that he had the next two days off and would stay in the building with his wife then.

Lillian was advised not to mention Chetwood's presence, as the officer installed himself in the manager's office from where he could hear anything going on in the public area of the savings and loan. A short time later, Lillian's sister came in to make a deposit. The sister asked, "Are you still alone here?"

Lillian said, "Yes, I'm alone. Jerry's still on vacation." Just then Chetwood coughed. The sister looked quizzically at Lillian who tried to cover by calling, "Oh, are you back?"

Chetwood responded, "Yeah. I'm here."

After the sister left, Lillian told Chetwood it was embarrassing, trying to explain why she had a man stashed in a side room without giving away the fact that he was a policeman.

Friday August 29

Walter Dewald told Officer Don Jasper that Kassow and Johnson were back in the savings and loan on Friday, the day after opening the small account. Dewald was sitting in the manager's office, reading a magazine, when his wife called, "Here they come again!" Dewald stayed in the office, but drew his gun and stood ready behind the door.

Johnson and Kassow dallied in the parking lot for about ten minutes, then went inside. The man who opened the account as Watterson Johnson told the teller he wanted to add his wife's name to the account.

She had asked him about that when he was in the day before, and at that time he said no. Now he was back.

Mrs. Dewald did the paperwork, and the men left. But they sat in the parking lot talking for about fifteen minutes before leaving.

While the two men sat in the car, Dewald told his wife to go to the curbside mailbox and try to get the license number while she pretended to pick up the mail, if she could do it without being seen. Lillian did as her husband suggested.

Dewald gave the license number and car description to Delhi police, telling Jasper that he expected a burglary because that's how the two men were known to police. Delhi agreed, and promised to stake out the place during the weekend.

Delhi police kept watch on the savings and loan, maintaining surveillance over the holiday weekend of August 30 through early morning of September 2.

Tuesday September 2

Bob Chetwood picked up a packet of pictures at the Delhi police station and drove around to Cabinet Supreme. The idea was to have Lillian Dewald look at the photos and see if she recognized anyone. Buried in the packet was a picture of Raymond Kassow. Police had that picture as a result of Kassow's previous arrest. There was no available picture of Johnson since he was a juvenile during all his arrests.

Lillian looked at the pictures and instantly pointed to the one of Kassow. "That's Watterson Johnson, the man who opened the account," she told Officer Chetwood.

"No," said Chetwood. "That's Raymond Kassow."

The teller replied, "Well, that's what he told me. He said his name was Watterson Johnson."

Some time later Kassow was asked why he had used Johnson's name, even signing it on the account form. "Just trying to be helpful," he said. Before he said that, Kassow had tried to convince police he had never been in Cabinet Supreme.

Later, Lillian remarked to her husband, Walter, "I wouldn't be surprised if Carl Ingle is involved in this."

Carl Ingle did maintenance work for manager Jerry Grueter on property which Grueter owned, and on some property owned by the savings and loan. Both Lillian and her husband knew that. Walter knew Grueter about as well as Lillian did. The two men sometimes went to the race track and did other things together.

Lillian's husband later told a Cincinnati police investigator that Grueter was angry about work that Ingle had not done, that he had threatened to fire his handyman. Walter Dewald told the investigator that Ingle also was upset because he wanted to buy one of Grueter's buildings, but at his price, not Grueter's.

Weekend of September 6-9

Delhi police surveillance was resumed that weekend, but nothing happened. Chetwood, Don Redman, John Eschenbach and Sgt. Tom Kollman took turns, watching from the top of the nearby Kroger building. There was a slight flurry in the middle of one night, when Kollman, on the roof of the grocery store, reported that someone was moving around the house next door to the savings and loan.

Jasper and Chetwood had positioned their cruiser on nearby Glen Oaks Drive when Kollman relayed his message on a hand-held radio. They made a thorough search of the entire area surrounding the savings and loan, but reported "negative results." Probably the nighttime wanderer was a neighbor, doing a late take-out-the-garbage chore. The stakeout continued to five-thirty in the morning on Tuesday of that weekend.

There had been two long weekends of night stakeout for the expected burglary. Another uneventful weekend passed, and Dewald decided he could relax. Manager Jerry Grueter was back from vacation and on the job. Lillian was no longer alone in the office.

Walter took a week off and went to Canada, returning on Tuesday, September 23, he later told Sgt. Russell Jackson, Cincinnati homicide investigator.

"I went to Canada for a week and then I came back, and a day later, this happened!" Dewald lamented.

Chapter Three

The Bloody Vault

11:14 am, Wednesday, September 24

Responding to the armed robbery report, Chief Makin and Officer Jasper arrived at the little thrift just behind the cruiser bearing Officers Eschenbach and Redman. The Delhi Life Squad came almost at the same time. Among squad members was Bob Chetwood, off duty as a policeman, but on duty as a volunteer life squad member. That put five members of the small department on the scene, with only two of them officially on duty, but all pumped up with free-flowing adrenaline.

As Makin rushed into the building, the first thing he saw was what Joe Huebner had seen—Lillian Dewald with her face in a pool of blood just beyond the vault door. Blood still was oozing from her nostrils and mouth, spreading out on the floor under and around her. Makin drew his breath in sharply. Like many area residents, he made mortgage payments at the savings and loan, and he had known Lillian for thirteen years.

Just back of that shocking sight were three other women "stacked up like beef in a slaughterhouse," one life squad member said. The vault floor was awash with blood. Makin stepped in and checked the first ankle he could reach, feeling for a pulse. There was none. He checked pulse points on the other women. There were none, nor was there any other sign of life. The head of the woman on top of the macabre pile rested on the head and shoulders of a woman beneath her, her legs towards the back of the vault.

The body of another woman was lying across the body of the third, her right cheek pressed up against a file cabinet, her eyeglasses shoved up on her forehead. Makin could see what appeared to be an entry wound over her right eye. She had bled extensively from the nose and mouth. Underneath her, visible from the bustline down, was a larger woman.

The chief stepped out of the vault and told Chetwood, "Call the county coroner's office and the Cincinnati Homicide Squad." Makin headed a small department with no experience in murder then, and certainly none in massacres. He knew he needed all the help he could get.

A deputy from the Hamilton County Sheriff's department drove up, telling Makin that Col. Paul Fricker and a lieutenant from the sheriff's department were en route. It was county communications which had broadcast the alarm, following Joe Huebner's phone call to a telephone operator who had alerted countywide Station X, the precursor to 911.

The man whose telephone call set all this in motion stayed quietly in front of the building lobby. He told Makin his wife was in the vault. He asked if everyone—his wife—was dead.

Yes, he was told. They were all dead.

11:27 am, Wednesday

Chief Makin directed Eschenbach to broadcast a "pick-up and hold for investigation of homicide" on Raymond Kassow and Watterson Johnson, the two men who had almost insistently called attention to themselves. The broadcast was just fifteen minutes after the first alarm went out, about twenty minutes after the four women were gunned down.

There was nothing in the known backgrounds of Kassow and Johnson to indicate they were capable of multiple homicide. Yet these two men had stood figuratively under that invisible but perceptible flashing neon sign which pointed to them.

11:45 am, Wednesday

Detectives Al Williamson and Charles Rutledge of the Cincinnati Homicide Squad came into the savings and loan, soon followed by three more investigators. They had to be escorted past the rope with which three cooperating law enforcement agencies had cordoned off the building.

A large crowd gathered. Mrs. Mary Ballman, a housewife who lived on nearby Anderson Ferry Road, came out of Kroger's where she had been grocery shopping. She was surprised to see ambulances parked on Delhi Pike. Curious, she walked over and saw a police car in the driveway at Cabinet Supreme. The door of the unoccupied cruiser was open and she could hear the police radio talking about a holdup and four homicides.

Four homicides! Mrs. Ballman felt as if she had been struck by a bolt of lightning. She stood with the gathering crowd of the curious, and heard a woman next to her say, "I wonder if anybody was hurt?" Mrs. Ballman replied, "Oh lady, there are four homicides!" She felt weak all over. She could hardly believe it. This kind of thing just didn't happen in Delhi.

She watched as life squad workers went into the building with stretchers, then saw them come out, the stretchers empty. Eyeing the empty stretchers, she realized no one would be going to the hospital. Feeling sick, Mary Ballman went home. As she put away her groceries, Mary thought, "That could have been me in there." She didn't bank at Cabinet Supreme, but sometimes accompanied friends on errands. Horrible. The word kept going through her mind like a litany. Horrible, horrible. Years later the woman still repeated the word almost compulsively every time she thought about what happened.

Inside, the experts from the Cincinnati Homicide Squad, a unit which boasted a 95 percent clearance rate, went to work. Williamson photographed everything, making a sweeping pictorial record. Detective Bill Dunn went out to look for anyone who might have seen or heard anything. Detectives Bernie Kersker and Bill Rathman searched every inch of the building, with Rutledge taking notes.

As Kersker and Rathman stepped into the red river in the vault, blood slopped over their shoes and socks and painted their ankles. They finally rolled up their trouser legs, trying to avoid blood splashes on their clothes as they searched for data. By the time they were finished, their feet were totally covered with blood.

There were blood splatters on Lillian Dewald's left leg. Two inches from her right foot was an ejected .25 caliber cartridge case. A footprint in the blood on the floor near her left elbow excited interest until it was discovered that it was made by a life squad member who had followed Makin into the building.

The woman on the bottom of the bloody pile later was identified as Mrs. Henrietta Stitzel, age sixty-four. Her feet were alongside the knees of Mrs. Dewald. Her head could not be seen because it was underneath the bodies of two other women. There was a large amount of blood on her right leg and blood splatters on her left leg. When the bodies were moved, a .25 caliber automatic casing was found under Henrietta.

The woman lying on top of Henrietta was her sister-in-law, Mrs. Luella Stitzel, age sixty-one. She lay across Henrietta's head and body, her head leaning flat against a metal filing cabinet to the left of the narrow vault, her feet resting on metal shelves on the other side. Luella's light gray horn-rimmed glasses were pushed up on her forehead, with blood showing on the left lens. She had a bullet wound in the left temple. There was a bloody stream which had run out of her mouth and nose down to the floor.

On top of this stomach-churning heap of women steeped in blood was the fourth victim, identified at the scene by her husband as Helen Huebner, age forty-six. Her head was turned to the left, and rested on the left leg of Luella Stitzel. She, too, had a bullet wound in the left temple. There was a bloody streak from her nose to her right ear, blood on her left shoulder and on the right front of the white sweater she wore. Blood spots and streaks showed inside her right knee. There was a .25 caliber automatic casing lying between her legs. The McAlpin's paycheck was still in its envelope, still in Helen's hand. She never had a chance to present it to Lillian Dewald to cash.

Investigators found a large pool of blood between the safe and filing cabinet on the left side of the vault where Lillian Dewald had sought futile refuge. One bullet had smashed through three nearby window screens leaning against the wall, shattering into nine fragments, eight of which fell to the floor. The ninth fragment was found lodged in one of the screens.

In all, five .25 caliber casings were found, four inside the vault and one on the outside of the open vault door. No women's purses were found, but Lillian Dewald's handbag later was discovered in a bottom drawer behind the counter.

Missing from the till was $111. Including money in the stolen handbags, police estimated total take at $275, or $68.75 per life.

Postmortem

Autopsies were underway within three hours of the robbery and shootings. Reports of the pathologists, Dr. Ben Yamaguchi and Dr. Khosrow Alamin, MD, relate in dreadful detail how life can end when least expected.

Mrs. Luella Stitzel, age sixty-one: Cause of death—intracranial hemorrhage due to gunshot wound of the head which lacerated the brain stem. Point of entry was 2.5 inches above the tip of the nose and .5 inch to the left of the midline. There was an exit wound at the back of the head 3 inches above the base of the neck, about 2 inches to the right of the midline.

Layman's translation: This woman experienced the terror of seeing her executioner aim the gun at her head and shoot her in the face. It was a horrifying final exit for the gentle, caring woman who had been a favorite with the neighborhood kids.

Mrs. Henrietta Stitzel, age sixty-four: Cause of death—intracranial hemorrhage due to gunshot wound of the head. Point of entry was 2.5 inches above the lateral terminus of the left eyebrow. The bullet went through the brain and exited .5 inch above the right ear. There also was a wound on the right index finger.

Layman's translation: The shooter gained control of his style, and aimed purposefully just above the temple and through the brain. The wound to the right index finger might indicate that Henrietta held her hand to her head in shock and fright. The bullet which passed through her brain could have nicked her finger on its way out.

The two women who had worked, played and prayed together also died together, and were together for a requiem high mass. They were buried in identical embossed doe-skin caskets in the old Catholic St. Joseph Cemetery on West Eighth Street in Price Hill, with Henrietta being laid to rest next to Matthew, who had been there for sixteen years.

When their car eventually was released to family, in the back seat was found a bag of goodies from Faultless Bakery, which had been a regular stop for them.

Mrs. Lillian Feist Dewald, age forty-one: Cause of death—internal hemorrhage due to multiple gunshot wounds. There were four entry wounds, all in the back, two of which were fatal. One bullet was found lodged in her right shoulder. A second bullet, found in the membrane that enfolds the lung, penetrated the left upper lobe of the lung and was fatal. One bullet penetrated the lower part of the intestine and was found lodged in tissues in front of the abdominal wall. The fourth bullet penetrated the pancreas and the liver, and exited through the right upper body in the front. That, too, was fatal. A spent slug was removed from her clothing at the site of the exit wound.

Layman's translation: This woman, whose body was found lying partially out of the vault, was shot four times in the back, although twice was enough to kill her. She screamed at her executioner and fought death, to no avail.

A police officer's wife and valued employee of Cabinet Supreme Savings and Loan for thirteen years, Lillian Dewald was one of fourteen children, descendants of an oldtime Delhi Township farm family. Bookkeeper and general factotum of the small thrift, she was liked and respected by the community in which she lived and worked. Following mass at St. Antoninus Church where she was a parishioner, Lillian was buried at Our Lady of Victory Cemetery.

Mrs. Helen Rischmann Huebner, age forty-six: Cause of death—intracranial hemorrhage due to gunshot wound to the head which lacerated parts of the brain. The entry wound was just above the left eyebrow to the side. The bullet was recovered from the right temporal muscle.

Layman's translation: The now experienced shooter reproduced the shooting of Henrietta. It was execution style, efficient and quick.

Helen was laid to rest in the cemetery of Our Lady of Victory Church where she was a member of the Christian Family Movement and Council of

Catholic Women which held prayers for her at the funeral home where her services were held.

The Brother

Walter Rischmann, on a break from his lithography job at a Cincinnati printing firm, walked into the company lunchroom and sat down at a table, vaguely aware of the radio playing in the corner. He heard a familiar name, and listened.

"Oh my god! That's my sister!" The newscaster had just named the shooting victims in the holdup at the Cabinet Supreme Savings and Loan. One was Walter's younger sister, Helen Rischmann Huebner.

A co-worker heard the exclamation, saw the stricken look on Rischmann's face, and asked, "What's the matter, Walt?" The thunderstruck brother could hardly talk. He pointed to the radio and tried to explain. It took a while.

Walter went to the phone. He needed to call home, to speak to his wife. He managed to dial. Ruth, who had just gotten home from a volunteer stint at their child's school, answered cheerfully. Walter tried to explain to his wife why he has calling, but by this time he was crying so hard he couldn't speak. The co-worker finally took the phone out of his hand and told Ruth her sister-in-law had been murdered.

Later that day, Rischmann was at the home of his brother-in-law, Joe Huebner, as Joe called the Virginia Beach Naval Base where his oldest son, Tom, with only seven days from the end of his hitch, was looking forward to going home. Joe told his son what had happened to his mother. Then he stood silently, the phone in his fist, an agonized expression on his face.

Walter asked, "What is it, Joe, what is he saying?"

Joe said not a word. Walter walked over, took the phone from Joe's inert hand and put it to his ear.

"The boy was just screaming and screaming," Walter said.

And at School

The kids at Our Lady of Victory School were in a buzz on Wednesday, September 24. They had heard about the holdup-murders at Cabinet Supreme, but did not know who had been shot. Danny Huebner, just thirteen years old, was called out of his eighth grade classroom and told to go over to the priest's house. The boy walked slowly to the rectory, wondering what he had done wrong. When he got there, the priest had picked up his Bible and was putting on his jacket. He said to the boy, "Sometimes things happen that we cannot understand" and other vague things that confused Danny.

The priest drove the boy home where his Uncle Walter and other relatives had gathered. Danny's father went to the boy and hugged him tight, but was crying too much to talk. It was then that the priest told the boy his mother was one of the women killed in the holdup the kids at school were talking about.

Danny never got over that moment.

Chapter Four

Johnny

Little Johnny France stood next to his mother, Ruby, at the window of their Over-the-Rhine apartment as they watched Claude France go into the raucous bar across the street. Claude was not alone, and Ruby was seething. It was not just that Claude was with another woman, although that was the focus of her anger. The building, with a restaurant on one side and the rowdy bar on the other, also was known for the hooker hangout on an upper floor. That building was no place for the father of a growing brood.

Ruby darted out of the apartment, ran across the street and went into the lounge. Seven-year-old Johnny followed his mother and watched through the door. He could see Claude and his female companion sitting at the bar. Ruby, who was just five feet one, charged up to Claude and swung. She punched the surprised man right off the barstool, knocking out one of his teeth. In the ensuing uproar Johnny scampered back to the apartment, wondering what was going to happen.

Police were not surprised to be summoned to the bar, known for its unruly clientele. Assault charges were filed against Ruby, and she was sentenced to six months in the Cincinnati Workhouse. The kids were sent to live with Grandma Burton on Klotter Street.

Of Johnny's brothers and sisters—eventually there would be thirteen of them—three bore the last name of France; eight were named Mitchell; two were named Cook. The first-born, Johnny's last name was France until he was about thirteen years old. Then he was arrested for shoplifting at Shillito's department store and was sent to Glenview School for Boys, a residential facility for troubled youth. His name for the record became John Leigh. That was the name on his birth certificate.

Having a different last name from any of his brothers and sisters bothered John. He had been Johnny France ever since he could remember, sharing a family name with three of his siblings. His dismal school record lists him as Johnny France, but his birth certificate says he is the son of Benjamin Harrison Leigh. John was Ruby's first child, and apparently there were no other Leigh children. John recalls no Benjamin Leigh in his childhood or at any time. "I can't even put a face with the name."

Before and after the incident which put the young mother in the Workhouse, Ruby and her mother, Rachel Burton, did what they could for all those children, but life was hard in the poverty ridden, crime beset Over-the-Rhine neighborhood. Ruby worked in a laundry during the day, sometimes in bars at night. One or another of the children was always sick. The oldest son made many trips to the hospital with his mother, sometimes walking through the snow to get a sick child there. It was the only way they knew to get medical treatment.

John says, "I can remember going to school without a coat in the winter." Nothing came easy, especially for the mother whose life was complicated by diabetes and heart problems.

Johnny honored school as much by his absence as his presence. His school records show he was average on such things as seriousness of purpose, industry and initiative, but his seventh grade marks mostly were abysmal. He wasn't there much. That year he was marked absent one-hundred days of a one-hundred-and eighty-day school year.

"In one door and out the other," he commented. "Used to play hooky a lot to go to the movie houses" where he didn't necessarily pay to get in. You could always get a friend to hold open the rear door of the theater. Didn't matter what the show was. For Johnny, any day at the movies was better than a day in school.

He did better in the eighth grade, missing only twenty-nine days. While he failed two of seven subjects, he drew a straight B average in math and did well in shop and art classes. Junior high was as far as Johnny got, except for a nighttime art class at Hughes High School, taken at the urging of a girl friend's brother-in-law, after the system had expelled him at age sixteen. He once had the satisfaction of seeing two of his pictures on display in a special exhibit at Taft High. The ability and interest in art remains, but has taken on a special slant.

After he got out of the Glenview juvenile home, Johnny stood on an Over-the-Rhine street corner with a needle, thread and ink tattooing the back of his fingers with the letters *L O V E*, as friends watched. When he got home, Grandma

Burton "smacked me upside my head" for the stupidity, but a fascination with tattoo art had been etched on his psyche as well as his skin.

Grandma Rachel Burton tried hard, giving her love and what little else she had, trying to impart values to the collection of grandkids turned over to her care, but some of them just wouldn't listen. Johnny ran the streets and cadged drinks at every opportunity. He got to know a lot of winos, an easy source of drink. They would buy a kid anything if given some money. A pint of Ripple or "Mad Dog," a sickly sweet wine, "was only about sixty-seven cents at the time, no big deal."

Johnny could get the money by using a mallet to knock off the heads of parking meters. That was usually good for four or five dollars. He developed a twisted respect for the way the street drinkers handled their cold weather housing problem.

"Winos ain't as dumb as people think they are. You never see many winos in the street in the wintertime. Ever wonder why? They know how to get six months in the Workhouse every year." The ancient (circa 1868) Workhouse (now replaced by the River City Correctional Center) looked like a ragged castle on the outside and smelled like an old dungeon on the inside. A visitor in its mess hall got a disquieting impression that some noxious thing was dead and rotting under the concrete floor. Winos thought of it as an almshouse, except that you had to break a law to gain entry. But it did offer food and a place to sleep. Three hots and a flop, in street parlance.

As Johnny grew, so did his alcohol problem. The stuff was easily available to those too young to get it legally. He knew a woman who worked in one of the neighborhood bars, who wasn't fussy about age. He paid in cash for very little of what he drank. Johnny learned that his growing sexual impulses were more than a private problem. It was a commodity. Sex was salable, or could be exchanged for other things.

In one saloon he met *Rex Miner, a man who showed him a world he knew nothing about, and eventually came to regret. Rex was a good-looking, blue-eyed blond, only a year older than Johnny, but years older in dissolute experience. A switch hitter, he taught Johnny that copulation could translate to cash in the gay world.

"We went to a lot of places together, but most of the time, once we got there we did our own thing. Rex would mess with anyone who he thought had some money or something he wanted," John said. "I was out to have a good time."

"Guess you could say most of his money came from other guys," John said. "We went to bars I would have never thought to go into at first. Always easy money to make in them. I was underage, but nobody cared."

Before he met Rex, Johnny was sixteen and running with a group of boys who formalized their friendship by calling themselves the Spiders. They signaled their connection with that ancient form of tribal marking, tattooing. They did this themselves, using a needle to puncture the skin in the form of a spider, overhung with a ribbon, then rubbing blue ink into the holes. At least one of the boys saw his arm blow up like a balloon from an infection caused by the painful and unhygienic amateur process.

The friendship, bonded in booze and bad judgment, was sometimes tested. Johnny was going with *Beryl, sister of Spider *Ben Blade, but he did it his way. As the two Spider buddies walked down the street one day, they saw Beryl and a couple of her girl friends about a block behind them. Johnny thought he was being spied on, and he didn't like it.

"If she's following me, I'm gonna kick her fucking ass," he said to Ben. He reckoned without family feeling. Ben faced Johnny and explained it to him. "You touch my sister and I'll kill you."

Johnny believed it. Ben was only fifteen and Johnny was sixteen, but the boys understood each other. They had been hanging out together since they were in Washington Park Elementary School. One of their joint enterprises had caused one shocked victim excruciating pain; another sent an innocent man to jail.

When the boys were barely pubescent and beginning to be fascinated by all things sexual, they combined that interest with larcenous intent and took to peeping in windows. Going down an alley between Republic and Race Streets, with Johnny showing off a newly acquired pellet gun to Ben, they noticed a window shade pulled down. The shade puller was in a careless hurry; there was about a four inch gap between the bottom of the shade and the window sill. The boys peeped. They saw a man with his trousers at half-mast, being serviced with fellatio, courtesy of one of the neighborhood ladies. The couple was only about three feet from the open window. Johnny couldn't resist. The target was too fascinating. He aimed the pellet gun and zinged the poor devil in his turgid private part.

"I never heard such a blood curdling scream in my entire life," said Ben. The boys ran like hell.

Johnny was really pleased with the pellet gun. "You could hit someone in the butt under water and it would still hurt. Used to shoot out a lot of street lights with it, and hall lights. The darker the better when you want to break into someplace in OTR [Over-the-Rhine.] What people can't see they can't ID."

When they were older, Johnny and Ben accompanied an elderly female relative to a Fifteenth Street bingo parlor, then wandered down the street and loitered. Ben leaned up against a parking meter, as they hung around, exchanging teenage witticisms. They saw a woman come out of the bingo parlor, clutching her purse. As the unsuspecting pigeon walked past the youths, Johnny reached out and grabbed her purse. The woman didn't take it lightly, fighting back, but she did take it lying down because that's where she was after Johnny punched her in the face to make her let go, and made off with the handbag.

Watching the street mugging from the window of a second floor apartment was an outraged twenty-two-year-old man who decided to be a hero. *Joe Samaritan swung out the window onto the fire escape and dropped at the feet of the woman, lying stunned on the ground. Ben was too surprised to move. Samaritan bore a striking resemblance to Johnny, including hair color and length, sideburns and a goatee.

Cops came. The woman pointed to her would-be rescuer and screamed, "It was him!" By this time Johnny, who had gone home, changed his shirt and slicked back his hair, came strolling casually up the street, wearing what he considered to be an air of innocence. "What's going on?" he asked.

The bruised and confused victim looked from Johnny to Samaritan and back again. "It was him! No! It was him!" The cops were disgusted. They checked backgrounds. Because Johnny was a juvenile, his record did not show, but Samaritan, who may have been choosy about his type of crime, nevertheless had a rap sheet for other offenses. He was charged, convicted and served time, Ben related. Ben was relieved that he was not caught up in the mess. For one thing, *he* knew who his father was and knew what his father's attitude would be if he were ever arrested.

A couple of years later, Ben was happily driving his newly acquired convertible and pulled up for a red light at the corner of Fourteenth and Vine. Out of nowhere, Johnny came running up and jumped into the automobile. He held a small metal box in his hand.

"Quick! Drive around the corner and down the street to the barber shop," he told Ben. Ben did what his friend asked. When Johnny came out of the barber shop, the sideburns and goatee were gone and his hair was shorter than Ben had ever seen.

Johnny explained. He knew a man who was reputed to keep a lot of money in his apartment, so Johnny recruited *Betty Lou, a large, economy-size female friend, to help him with a get-rich-quick scheme. Betty Lou would make sexual overtures to the money man and keep him occupied in the bedroom while Johnny scouted the rest of the apartment. It worked. The box Johnny found and stole had $1,700 in it. From this treasure trove he gave Ben a $100 bill for his trouble. What, if anything, Betty Lou got out of it is unknown.

With a pocket full of stolen cash, Johnny decided it might be wise to get out of town for a while. He went to Rick, a friend who drove a soda pop truck for a living, and talked him into taking a hitchhiking holiday to California. The two men thumbed their way west on Route 66 and I-40. It was a harbinger of Johnny's future when he would take the same route as a fugitive from a murder charge.

They got to Los Angeles, looked around and Johnny decided this was not his kind of city. "L.A. was too fast for me," he said. "You walk down a downtown street and every few feet, somebody is pressuring you for sex, or to buy porno stuff or drugs." They stayed only two days, then hitched back to Cincinnati. There they both found work in a plastic bag factory, although for Johnny, the job would last only six weeks.

Meanwhile, Ben had taken stock and decided that Johnny's life style was fraught with hazard. He could see eventual prison time looming, and wanted to get out before he got in. He cooled the friendship. Johnny France, alias John Leigh, went on to bigger things.

Chapter Five

The Man

In 1969 the Delhi Police Department boasted seven officers including the chief. Howard R. Makin had been with the township department for nine years, chief for seven.

The boy who grew up on Wilder Avenue, more than two decades later would touch the lives of two families on nearby Denver Street, although he knew none of them as a child. Makin would come to know the victimized family of Henrietta and Luella Stitzel, and of Raymond Kassow, malefactor.

Howard attended Blessed Sacrament grade school at the corner of Wilder and Denver, in the parish where the Stitzels went to mass. Ironically, as a boy, he was sent to get his hair cut in the shop at Neave and River Road, where Ray Kassow's father was the barber.

Because his mother died of a ruptured appendix when he was just one year old, like John Leigh young Makin was raised by his grandmother. His father remarried, and like John Leigh he had half-brothers. Makin's brothers would grow up to be businessmen and professionals. Many of Leigh's brothers would wind up in jail.

Like John Leigh, Howard Makin would learn many things from an array of relatives. The things they learned were as different as their families were dissimilar. As a boy, John Leigh was taken to visit one uncle at London Correctional Institution. With another uncle he was going from bar to bar learning how to drink and how to get into brawls. Howard Makin's uncles taught him to

43

play baseball and football, how to fish and hunt. Amused family members told him that his late mother wanted him to grow up to be either a baseball player or a gangster.

Makin and Leigh both would become men with guns, on opposite sides of the law.

Grandma Makin was close to her grandson and delighted him with stories of her father riding with Morgan's Raiders, the Confederate cavalry squadron whose forays reached into Ohio and marched through Cincinnati suburbs. He lived with Grandma Makin until he was married at the age of twenty.

Wanting more than anything to become a Cincinnati police officer, young Makin did not quite make the minimum height requirement, so he went to work selling electronic parts, then life insurance. That was interrupted when he was drafted during the Korean War.

The army sent Makin to the Adjutant General School at Fort Benjamin Harrison, Indiana where a large part of the curriculum was military law. Because the eight previous graduating classes were sent to Korea, Makin believed that would be his fate, but he was surprised. His entire class was assigned stateside. Makin was sent to Fifth Army Headquarters in Chicago.

"My boss was a first lieutenant, but he was without doubt the most powerful first lieutenant in the army," Makin said. "He was the guy who decided the assignment of every GI in the Fifth Army, including sending troops overseas wherever needed. He received a lot of phone calls from senators and congressmen attempting to get a favorable assignment for a constituent. He wanted every phone conversation recorded and transcribed."

That was Makin's job. He had learned shorthand and typing. He recalled transcribing conversations with Senators Estes Kefauver and Everett Dirksen, among other notables. It was a liberal education.

Seven months later an army time-study team analyzed Makin's slot out of existence. His lieutenant told him to decide where he wanted to go, so Makin took a two week furlough to think about it. Home in Cincinnati, he learned there was a military police detachment right across the river in Fort Thomas, Kentucky, and he decided that was it. As it happened, the Fort Thomas detachment was based in Fort Hayes in Columbus, Ohio, so Makin's orders were cut for Fort Hayes, with subsequent assignment to Fort Thomas.

He never got to Fort Thomas. His new boss, provost marshal for the state of Ohio, had other ideas. The major thought it would be great to have his own stenographer to transcribe hearings which would determine whether some local bars should be placed off limits.

Said Makin, "In the eight months I was there he never had such a hearing. So I spent my time traveling around central and northern Ohio picking up AWOL servicemen." These wanderers were brought to Fort Hayes, then put on a bus for Fort Knox, Kentucky, every Friday evening.

Makin said, "If possible I would get a guard assignment on the bus, and then get off in Cincinnati on the way back from Fort Knox. That way I was home early Saturday morning and didn't have to be back in Columbus until Sunday night."

He added, "Compared to other things one could be doing, this was a gravy assignment."

At the time he hated the army. It had disrupted his life, but he found his assignments interesting. In retrospect, Makin concluded "there is a lot to be learned serving a hitch in the service. We might have a much improved younger generation if there was such a thing as mandatory military service right out of high school for two years." For Makin, the time spent in a military police detachment enhanced his earlier desire to be a police officer.

After discharge from the army, Makin returned to selling life insurance and electronic parts. He moved his family (by this time, he had two daughters) to Delhi Township where a story in the local newspaper rekindled his longstanding interest in police work. Delhi was about to start its own police department. He applied, got the job and two years later, he was chief.

The new Delhi department started in June 1961 with just three part-time men. The township was protected by the Hamilton County Sheriff's department, and the new police force began as a supplement to the sheriff's patrol. When Makin was named chief in 1963, there were three full-time officers and one part-timer. By 1969 there were seven full-time sworn personnel. One year later the department was autonomous, independent of the sheriff's department. The Delhi department eventually grew to twenty-seven full-time sworn personnel.

Makin is a quiet man, composed and deliberate. His leadership style gives the troops something to think about. An embarrassing moment for Sergeant John ("call me Satch") Coletta became words to remember.

One less than proud moment in his Delhi career, Sergeant Coletta says, is when he was a plain clothes investigator, cooperating with Cincinnati police to find a house burglar operating in both their areas.

The wily thief was elusive until he expanded into an Indiana county just west of the Ohio line. Ohio police followed the man into Hidden Valley, Indiana where they separated, keeping in touch by radio. Some followed the thief to Elm Street while Coletta drove to the local golf course, asking for an Indiana officer to meet him in an unmarked car.

The Indiana cop car "did not have any decals on it, but it looked like the rolling Voice of America," Coletta said. "The guy inside was in uniform with patches showing on the shoulder." Delhi and Cincinnati detectives were all in plain clothes. Coletta took off his jacket and asked the Indiana man to put it on. He asked where Elm Street was. The man didn't know. Coletta's partner informed him by radio that it ran off Lakeview, a main street in Hidden Valley.

"I asked the Indiana guy where Lakeview was and he didn't know that, either," Coletta said. "With that, I blew up and called him some bad names. I told him it was no wonder they are breaking into your houses; you don't even know the streets."

But the two police factions did join forces at a point where the thief had already broken into one house and "was inside another when we surrounded the place and called his name, telling him to come out." The thief came out. Discovering "we were Ohio police, he asked if we had the authority to arrest him in Indiana. At that point I asked for my jacket back." The Indiana officer took it off, and with his insignia showing, identified himself as the chief deputy of Dearborn County.

Recalling all the choice names he had called the deputy, Coletta said, "I wanted to pass out immediately. He asked for cards from all the officers involved. I really didn't want to give him mine, but I did. When I got back to Delhi I went to see Chief Makin and asked him if a telephone call had beaten me back to Delhi."

"Should it have?" Makin asked. Coletta explained. The chief listened to the abashed cop, then said, "A policeman is often remembered more for what he says than what he does." The deputy didn't call, and a lot of stolen property was recovered as a result of that arrest. And Coletta never forgot his chief's response.

Makin's case notes reveal a professional, almost detached approach to evidence gathering, even in the face of horror. The events of September 24, 1969 left an indelible mark on him. Essentially a gentle man, he walked into the savings and loan to find a bloody mess—four dead women lying in pools of blood, one of them an acquaintance of many years.

At the time of the sensational crime at Cabinet Supreme, Makin told the press that he asked for help from other police agencies because "I am not an expert in this field." Three years later he attended the 91st session of the FBI National Academy at Quantico, Virginia. Later he would send to the academy Lt. John Eschenbach, now a thirty-one year police veteran, and also Capt. Tom Bauer.

Eschenbach, who has been with the Delhi department since 1965, knows a side of Makin not generally seen by the public. "This man will always be my friend, but he'll never be my car partner again," Eschenbach once said of Makin. He explained why.

"We had been to an FBI retraining session in Columbus and were on our way back to Delhi," Eschenbach said. They were passing through Reynoldsburg, a Columbus suburb.

"We'd had a few—apple juice drinks, I guess." He grinned.

"I was driving. All of a sudden this Reynoldsburg policeman comes across the median, blue lights flashing. I was going a little over the speed limit, I guess. Of course I pulled over." He gestured towards Makin. "This man here was sitting with a gin and tonic in his hand.

"As the Reynoldsburg officer approached, Makin jumps out of the passenger side of the car and says, 'Am I glad to see you! I've just been kidnapped and this man has a gun.'

"At this point, the Reynoldsburg officer is reaching for *his* gun." Eschenbach paused. "I thought Oh, God! This is going downhill. But eventually, the officer caught the idea. He took the humor of the situation and sent us on our way. I was grateful for it. He couldn't believe us, I guess."

And that, Eschenbach concluded, is why Makin will never again be his car partner.

Captain Bauer has been with the department for twenty-one years. One of the new breed of educated cops, Bauer has two degrees in criminal justice, a bachelor's and a master's. He sees more education as the wave of police future. But it was the growing reputation which came out of the Cabinet Supreme case that drew him to the small Delhi department when he was a student at the University of Cincinnati, after three years in the army. Under Makin's leadership, "we have prepared ourselves for the future," Bauer says.

With satisfaction, Chief Makin comments, "Not too many departments our size have three graduates from the West Point of law enforcement," referring to the FBI National Academy.

Makin's tenure as police chief is lauded by his employers, past and present. In an age when it is popular pastime to take potshots at police, the Delhi Department draws plaudits.

"Makin built one of the top departments in the area at a time when township police were under constant challenge from the sheriff's patrol who saw them as direct competition," said W. Emerson "Dusty" Rhodes, former township trustee, who is now Hamilton County auditor. "He is steady and professional," Rhodes continued, "an excellent leader who created an unmatched *esprit de corps.*"

John Artmayer, another former trustee, now retired from his job as a principal in the Oak Hills School District, said "Makin built a department on sound police principles. He always did a professional job."

Current Trustee Carol Espelage reiterated those feelings, saying the entire board feels the same. She added, "I have the highest regard for Chief Makin and every man in that department."

Makin has been described by Ohio law enforcement officials as "the cornerstone for building unified, cooperative efforts among the numerous police agencies of Hamilton County."

As a young police department, Delhi was grateful for the help it got when it had a spectacular crime on its hands. Makin guided his growing department to provide the kind of help and cooperation which it had received.

His peers share public perception of Makin's leadership capabilities. He is one of only two men to serve three terms as president of the Hamilton County Police Association. He was twice elected president of the county Police Chiefs Association, and twice served as chairman of the Regional Computer Information Center, which networks with the National Crime Information Center.

The definitive statement came from retired Cincinnati police detective Bernie Kersker who was an investigator in the crime at Cabinet Supreme.

Kersker said, "Makin is one sharp copper. He did everything right."

Chapter Six

Marshaling the Manhunt

After four hours at Cabinet Supreme, Chief Makin drove back to Delhi police headquarters on Neeb Road. As he walked wearily into the building, Sergeant Kollman stopped him and told him that Raymond Kassow had been picked up by two Cincinnati officers, and was being held in a back room.

The stationhouse was teeming with people, many of whom were off-duty officers who heard the news and came to offer assistance. Some were in shorts and T-shirts, men who just shut off their lawn mowers or turned off the television, got in their cars and went to help. With on-duty officers from the county, from Cincinnati and Delhi it made quite a crew, about forty men. There also was a gaggle of both print and video press reporters.

The press was put on hold while a briefing was held for officers. Men were assigned to do a door-to-door, house and store canvass, seeking possible witnesses. Others were told to check out area motels, restaurants and bars. They scattered, and Makin turned his attention briefly to the press, giving them what he could.

Tied up with lawmen and news people, Makin reacted testily when Officer Don Redman came to him and said, "Chief, Ron Carr is outside and wants to talk to you. He won't tell me why, but says it's important."

"It had better be," Makin snapped. "I don't have time for small talk." He asked sheriff's Lt. Herb Vogel to begin the interview with Kassow, and went outside to the parking lot where Carr waited.

Ronald Carr, age twenty-two, was a native of Lower Price Hill, then living in a Delhi apartment. He worked for a local building contractor. Carr paced back and forth in the police parking lot, holding a set of house plans in his hand. Makin greeted him with "Ron, I'm a little bit busy here."

The young man replied, "Chief, I have to tell you something. About a week ago I was in the police station and I saw a picture of Ray Kassow hanging on the bulletin board." Makin frowned. So what?

Carr explained, "I didn't say anything at the time because I wasn't sure I should be reading police bulletin board stuff, but I know Ray Kassow. We grew up in the same neighborhood. That's why his picture caught my eye." The picture was on the FIR which John Eschenbach had posted August 3, after stopping Kassow and Johnson on their middle of the night tour of Goodwill boxes.

"Ray's dad was a barber, had a shop near where we lived," Carr said. "Ray was a mean guy then, and all the kids in the neighborhood were afraid of him. He used to kill cats and he bullied everybody." Makin listened impatiently.

"Anyway, this morning I stopped at Frisch's for breakfast, and to pick up my lunch for the day," Carr continued. Frisch's is the restaurant to the left of Cabinet Supreme. A chain link fence divided the Frisch's parking lot from a section of the Kroger parking lot, just beyond which was the savings and loan. Carr told Makin he pulled his pickup truck into the Frisch's lot, parking next to the fence, and noticed that the car just on the other side of the fence was a convertible. It was backed into the fence, facing the savings and loan. "That was between 9:00 a.m. and 9:30 a.m.," Carr said.

"I turned off my motor and started to get out," Carr continued, "and that's when I saw Ray Kassow. He was in the passenger side of the convertible." Carr told the chief that as he looked, he saw another man get out of the driver's seat.

Carr remembered Kassow, not fondly, from childhood. He also remembered seeing Ray's picture on the police bulletin board. Because of those memories he jotted down the license number of the convertible on a set of house plans laying on the front seat of his truck. That was what he now held in his hand.

Later, Makin said, "I could have kissed him. This was a tremendously vital piece of information. It put Kassow in the immediate area of the crime, close to the time the crime was committed." It also provided an accurate license number. Joe Huebner's hasty glance at the convertible tags earlier that day was flawed by what the man was going through. This was specific, no guesswork. This number, Ohio 5244 AH, also would connect a third man with the crime.

"I went into Frisch's, and when I came back out, the convertible was gone," Carr told the chief. When Carr heard the news of the holdup, he realized he had to go see police right away. Carr would become a key witness in the investigation.

4:50 pm, Wednesday

Hamilton County Sheriff's Deputy Vogel spent about an hour with Kassow in the back room of the Delhi department, then came out, saying he was making no progress. Kassow denied having been in Delhi that day, adding he had "not been out that way for a number of weeks." He denied ever having been in the Cabinet Supreme Savings and Loan building.

Second man at bat with Kassow was Gus Feldman, an expert interviewer with Cincinnati's Criminal Investigation Section. Feldman came close to getting Kassow to admit involvement, but never quite got him over the edge. Kassow did say he owned a .22 revolver and a .22 rifle, but denied owning any other weapon. While Kassow was busy denying everything except that the grass was green, another scenario was in progress.

The township road foreman and an architect were measuring the back of the building, which included a window in the room where Kassow was being questioned. Makin shooed them away and took Ron Carr back there under pretext of continuing the window measurement. Carr looked through the window and identified Kassow as the man he had seen in the convertible with license plate 5244 AH earlier that day. Carr commented, "He's changed his clothes from what he was wearing this morning."

7:28 pm, Wednesday

Makin left Vogel and Feldman to talk with Kassow and went to the telephone in his office. He initiated a computer search on license plate 5244 AH. He ordered food brought in for the prisoner, and while he was at it, he contacted Judge Rupert Doan.

Doan then was on the municipal court bench for the municipal-county court system in Hamilton County. (He later became an appellate court judge.) One of Makin's men earlier told him that Judge Doan, a Delhi resident, could be contacted, if needed, on the local golf course. Makin made the contact, asking for a search warrant for Kassow's Denver Street home, based on the man's admission of owning a .22 revolver. Such a weapon had been used in the shootings. Doan went to the police station, and the warrant was signed.

While the search warrant was put to use, conversation with the prisoner continued, lasting until 9:30 p.m. when Kassow suddenly asked to be allowed to take a polygraph test. The interview ended abruptly.

Police later speculated that Kassow naively thought the polygraph test might help him because once before it had cleared him in a theft with which he had been charged. Makin called Cincinnati to arrange for the test and was told to bring his prisoner downtown to the crime bureau in about an hour.

About the same time Kassow was taken to the Cincinnati Crime Bureau, Makin learned that the search of the prisoner's house had turned up the .22 caliber revolver he said he owned. It also turned up a .22 automatic pistol and a .25 automatic pistol, neither of which he had mentioned. Asked why, the man who was being questioned about multiple murders coyly responded he thought it might be against the law to own an automatic, and he didn't want to get into trouble.

The search of Kassow's house also turned up a stolen Underwood electric typewriter. The serial number on the typewriter matched the serial number on a typewriter reported stolen August 14 from Santa Maria Neighborhood House, a settlement house in Lower Price Hill. Carl Ingle, the handyman mentioned by Lillian and Walter Dewald, sometimes did repair and maintenance work for Santa Maria. Edward Domit, director of the settlement house, told police that Ingle had a key to the building, but the burglary apparently was the result of an unlocked window. Domit said while he knew Ingle only casually, he had great faith in him.

11:00 pm, Wednesday

The polygraph examination requested by Ray Kassow began at 11 p.m. the day of the holdup, and ended at 12:15 a.m. the start of the new day, September 25.

Polygraph specialist Hugh Burger asked Kassow five key questions.

1. "Do you know for sure who robbed the Cabinet Supreme Building and Loan?"
   Answer: "No."
2. "Did you rob the Cabinet Supreme Building and Loan?"
   Answer: "No."
3. "Do you know for sure who shot the women at the Cabinet Supreme Building and Loan?"
   Answer: "No."
4. "Did you shoot the women at the Cabinet Supreme Building and Loan?"
   Answer: "No."
5. "Have you told us the entire truth as to your knowledge of the robbery at the Cabinet Supreme Building and Loan ?"
   Answer: "Yes."

Kassow asserted he was telling the truth on all matters. The polygraph examiner did not agree. Burger reported, "It is the opinion of the examiner . . . that he was not telling the truth" on most of the questions.

The one exception was "Did you shoot the women?" Burger said that because of "mixed and erratic emotional disturbances" he "could not render an opinion as to this person's truthfulness" on question four.

The examiner said that three individual tests were given, that "Kassow reacted (indicating falsehood) to all crime questions with the exception of the question on actually shooting the women." Burger told Chief Makin and other officers he "was certain Kassow was involved" and he asked permission to interrogate the man. That questioning went from 12:45 a.m. to 1:45 a.m. during which, Burger reported, "Kassow would never deny the robbery, but would only state that he did not do the shooting. He kept repeating, 'I could never do anything like that! Check my record.'"

At quarter to two in the morning, Burger told investigators, "Kassow is psychologically worn out and I don't believe further testing would produce any results."

Burger also said Kassow asked to talk with his wife, Betty. Two officers were sent to the Kassow residence to pick up the young woman and bring her to the crime bureau where she was allowed a private visit with her husband. They were still talking when Makin left for home at 4:30 a.m. It had been a long day.

While Kassow was being viewed and reviewed, the computer search on the license plate number supplied by Ron Carr turned up the name of one Graham Davis of Renner Street. Also turned up at Cincinnati Police District Five was an auto larceny report filed by Davis on the day of the holdup.

Davis told an officer that his car, a blue Chevrolet Malibu convertible, was taken from in front of his home between 10:30 a.m. and 5:30 p.m. The complaint was not filed until 8:30 p.m., one hour after Makin requested registration information on the vehicle. The officer taking the theft report was at pains to note that Davis had waited three hours to file a complaint after concluding his car had been stolen. That was well after the Delhi crime had hit the news.

Informed of the car theft report, Makin instantly asked that when and if found, the vehicle be preserved for a fingerprint check.

Rita Leigh

Police walked and talked to people along Renner Street, trying to find out if anyone saw the Davis car taken. They stopped in at the Davis apartment, and there they found Rita Carol Leigh, the twenty-year-old wife of a man named John Levi Leigh.

Rita's roots were in Pine Knot, Kentucky, near the Tennessee state line. Of his childlike bride with the flowing brown hair, who at twenty looked more like a fifteen-year-old, John Leigh said, "She was just a good ol' hillbilly gal who really didn't know much about the big city."

Rita's innocence was a source of fun to Johnny and their friends, Stella and Troy, who were all about the same age, but they were eons older in experience. One night when Troy, a biker, was out carousing with the Iron Horsemen, Johnny and Stella took Rita to a gay bar just to watch her reaction.

As they settled into a booth in the dimly lit bistro, the waitress strolled over. A tall good-looking brunette with a Peter Pan haircut, she wore a man-tailored uniform and a friendly smile. "Hi!" she greeted Johnny and Stella, staring at Rita. "Who's the little cutey?" Rita blushed.

"That's my wife," Johnny told the waitress. The woman raised her eyebrows, then shrugged. "Oh, well, no harm in trying." Johnny and Stella laughed. The waitress took their drink orders and left. Rita realized something was a little different here, and Johnny and Stella snickered at her confusion. Rita still didn't really understand when the waitress, who wasn't totally discouraged, kept bringing her free drinks. Unlike her young husband, Rita wasn't much of a drinker and she just passed them to her companions.

John reminisced, "I believe I was sixteen when I met Rita, and seventeen when we got married. Her mom and dad were dead. She was living with her sister and brother-in-law when I met her on Klotter Street." He reflected, "My marriage at the time I thought was the greatest thing going, but I wasn't ready for it—couldn't take care of myself, let alone a wife. I did love her and feel like a real asshole, even today, for letting her down."

John Leigh was only twenty years old, too, but the young couple already had been married for three years. It was a difficult time, with John and Rita bouncing from place to place, where ever they could put a roof over their heads. Most recently they had been on Wheeler Street for three months with their friends, Stella and Troy. Before that, it was three months on Klotter Street with John's grandmother. When John and Rick got back from California, the couple found a place on Ohio Avenue where they lived for five months.

Mostly, John was unemployed, but while they were in the Ohio Avenue apartment, both John and Rita found work with a company that made plastic bags. John operated a machine which sealed the bags until the day he got into an argument with his supervisor when he was late for work. John figured he had a good reason for being late. The parking brakes on his old car had apparently failed and it rolled off one of Cincinnati's hills, leaving him with a transportation problem. The supervisor wasn't interested in details and the discussion got heated. John was fired. Rita quit. They had been there just six weeks.

A month and a half later, when the television screen flashed John's picture because he was wanted in connection with the Cabinet Supreme robbery and murders, the plant manager was watching with other plant employees. "My God!" the manager exclaimed, "That guy used to work for us." Police spoke with plant personnel, but did not learn anything else they didn't already know.

The day police stopped at the Renner Street apartment when they were seeking clues about the missing Davis car, Rita Leigh told officers that she was at Graham's apartment to ask if he had seen her husband. "The last time I saw Johnny was about quarter to eight this morning when he came home," she said. He had been out all night, she said.

"Did John come home alone?" police asked.

"No, he was with a big red-headed guy I don't know. They only stayed about five minutes, then they left," Rita said. John told her he would be back about noon, to take her to the bus station to visit her grandmother in Pine Knot, she said. "What kind of car did they leave in?" police asked.

"I don't know. I was in bed. I didn't see the car." Rita said Johnny didn't come home at noon. She didn't know where he was.

With Rita Leigh in the Davis apartment police found two other persons. They were Stella Perkins, age 20, of the same Wheeler Street address as the Leighs, and a man who gave his name as David France, of a Pleasant Street address which was the home of John Leigh's mother, Ruby Mitchell. France turned out to be John Leigh's younger brother, also known as Dave Mitchell. Other finds in the Davis apartment raised a couple of police eyebrows. There were nude photos of John Leigh and a man named Troy Roark. Stella said Troy was her boy friend. Stella said she and Troy and the Leighs all lived together on Wheeler Street.

Stella told police the last time she saw John Leigh was about eight o'clock that morning, in a car in front of the Wheeler Street house. "Johnny was talking with this guy they call Red." She described the car as a dark blue Chevrolet Malibu with a white convertible top, which she said was owned by a guy named Dave. Pressed, she elaborated that "Dave" was Graham Davis, "but we call him Dave."

Stella said Johnny and Red left together in the convertible, that she didn't see them after that. She identified a picture of Raymond Kassow as a one-time visitor to their home, along with Red and Johnny.

While Cincinnati police were out looking for the car in which Delhi police had become interested and which the owner reported stolen, the missing vehicle was discovered in the Queen City Chevrolet parking lot on West Court Street in downtown Cincinnati. It was towed to a police impoundment lot and held until it could be checked out by fingerprint specialists and other investigators. It would be four months before Davis got his car back.

Davis was interviewed that night about eleven o'clock. He told police he loaned his car to John Leigh from time to time, but adamantly denied giving him permission to use the car that day.

The next day Troy Roark was questioned by County Detective Bill Breitfelder and Delhi Sgt. Tom Kollman, both involved in the murder investigation. Roark told the officers that on September 24 John Leigh went to the home of his brother,

Dave, to change clothes "because his were covered with blood." Roark said Leigh and Watterson Johnson left Cincinnati Wednesday night in an old blue Dodge owned by Leigh's uncle, "Boots" Burton.

Roark also said Leigh had called his grandmother's house that Thursday morning, asking his uncle to contact his wife at Roark's place, get his clothes and bring them to Pine Knot. Roark said Leigh's brother, Dave, Rita and Leigh's Uncle Boots "moved Johnny's belongings out of my apartment" that day, September 25.

Uncle Boots

Richard Vernon "Boots" Burton, age forty-two, was John Leigh's maternal uncle, who lived on Klotter Street with his mother, Rachel Burton, John Leigh's grandmother. Uncle Boots was sought out and interviewed by Delhi's Sergeant Kollman.

Burton told Kollman that on the afternoon of September 24, his nephew, Johnny, and Watterson Johnson came to him and asked him to drive them to Kentucky. Burton said he agreed. He drove the men to Lexington, and dropped them off near a Greyhound bus station. They gave him gas money so he could get back to Cincinnati, he said, saying they were going to Pine Knot. Burton said he got home about 7:00 p.m.

About six o'clock the next morning, Burton said, he picked up John's wife, Rita, and drove her to Pine Knot. He did not see Leigh or Johnson.

Sergeant Kollman had done his homework. He discovered that Uncle Boots had an arrest record of twenty-three misdemeanors and two felonies, plus a lengthy string of traffic arrests dating back to 1947. Kollman suggested that Burton be considered an accessory before and after the fact because of "his plea of ignorance as to why Leigh and Johnson wanted to get out of town" and because he had provided the second escape car after the robbery and homicides. Uncle Boots was not charged, but police regarded him with well-deserved interest.

Richard Vernon Burton's record ranged from contributing to the delinquency of a minor to eight separate counts of assault and battery. It included two counts of malicious destruction of property, three of disorderly conduct and four of public intoxication.

The "contributing" charge could have been related to his friendship with his young nephew. John Leigh said, "I used to go to bars with him a lot when I was a kid. Boots liked to hang out in bars, and he got into them knife fights. He was absolutely terrible at it—used to get beat up a lot. He had quite a few scars."

All things considered, police thought they would talk to Uncle Boots at greater length. A couple of days later he was questioned again, this time by

Cincinnati's homicide experts, Sgt. Russell Jackson, then a twenty-eight-year police veteran and chief of the homicide squad, and Detectives Oberschmidt and Morgan.

It was a cat and mouse game, with the questioners pawing Burton this way and that, ready to pounce on each evasion. Uncle Boots was not in the habit of being straightforward with police, but these officers had been there before. Somewhere in the evasions, they knew, was the possibility of real information, something that might help them find the men they sought. The question and answer session was a revealing portrait of the man.

Burton told the detectives that Johnny "just asked me to take them across the river."

"Did he say where across the river?"

"No, sir. Just right across the river."

"And what did you say?"

"I said okay."

"And so when you went across the river, did you drive or did somebody else drive?"

"No, sir. Johnny drove."

"And what way did you drive?"

"He went across that bridge down there. I don't know which one, but he went across that one bridge down there. The old bridge is blocked off."

"You said before that you stopped somewhere to get something to eat."

"He did."

"Was that here in Cincinnati?"

"No, sir. It was on Twenty-seven."

"Where on Twenty-seven?"

"I couldn't tell. I don't know the restaurant's name."

"Well now, I thought that you said before you went down the expressway?"

"He did go down the expressway."

"The expressway is I-75."

"I know it's I-75."

"How did you get on Twenty-seven?"

"Well I—he—didn't get on Twenty-seven. He took the expressway all the way down to Lexington."

"I see. And you didn't stop and get something to eat until you got past Lexington, then?"

"No. He got something to eat before he got to Lexington. He took a bypass somewhere."

"He got off I-75 and got on Twenty-seven?"

"He got on a bypass and stopped at a restaurant."

"Where at?"

"I couldn't say what town it was."

"All right. And the three of you got something to eat there?"

"Yes, sir."

"Where did you take them in Lexington?"

"I didn't take them nowhere. Johnny just drove a couple of blocks up from the street, to the bus station."

"Down in Lexington?"

"Yes, sir."

"All right. How much money did they give you for doing this?"

"I got four dollars when I left there."

"Did they fill up your tank, though?"

"They had gas in the car."

"I know they had gas in the car, but did they put the gas in and pay for it?"

"Yeah, they paid for it. Yes sir, they did."

"Where did they tell you they were going?"

"They told me they were going down in Kentucky, around Pine Knot, because his wife was supposed to be down there."

"Well, why didn't you drive them to Pine Knot?"

"Cause I wasn't in no shape to drive all the way back, what shape I was in." Pine Knot was about 100 miles further south in the state, near the northern border of Tennessee.

"What kind of shape were you in?"

"My legs and my hip was bothering me and that's how come I couldn't drive them across the river."

"So then what happened?"

"After I took them to Lexington, I came straight back home."

"Did they tell you where they were going?"

"No sir, they didn't tell me where they was going. But his wife supposed to leave, though, about this Sunday, to go to Pine Knot."

"And then later on, you took the wife of Johnny Leigh down to Lexington? Is that true?"

"Yes sir. I sure did. I took her to—"

"When did you do that?"

"I took her to Pine Knot. That's Thursday afternoon."

"And why did you do that?"

"Because she said that her grandma was sick. And she asked me to take her down there."

"Did she also say she was going to meet her husband down there?"

"No, she didn't say anything about meeting her husband."

"Where are you from, originally?"

"Raised and born right here in Cincinnati."

"Where're your folks from?"

"My mom's from Kentucky, Columbia, Kentucky."

"Are you married?"

"Yes sir."

"You have some children?"

"I ain't get—got my divorce from my wife, but I'm still married to her."

"You still have some children?"

"Yes sir."

"How many children do you have?"

"I got four by her."

"But she has the children?"

"Yes."

"You're not supporting them?"

"She's got two of them. No sir."

"You're not supporting them?"

"No sir. I got four of them by her. I got two of them's married, and the other two, I don't know where they're at."

"How old are you?"

"I'll be forty-three this coming December."

"And you're living here with your mother?"

"Yes sir."

"What's your phone number there?"

"I got my bill, but I couldn't tell you the number."

"You don't know the number?"

"No sir; not right off hand."

Police were exasperated. After some further discussion, a detective remarked, "When an officer first asked you about it, you denied driving them anywhere."

"I didn't drive them. He drove."

"You're getting technical now. You denied even seeing them."

"Yeah. I'll own up to that. Yeah."

"Okay, so you did lie to the police at that time? Why did you do that?"

"I didn't want to get him in no trouble. I didn't know what he's wanted for."

"How could this get him into trouble, if you tell where he is, that you saw him before? How could this get him into trouble?"

"I don't know."

"You didn't want him to get caught, in other words."

"No, I don't want nobody to get caught if they can get away. I mean, if I knew it was all that bad, I was sure, I'd sure turn him in, but I had the car—"

"Yeah, I'm sure you would."

"If he had called me, if I'd a knew where he was at, I'd tell you."

"Okay. Thank you very much."

"After he—if he done me that dirty—"

That was John Levi Leigh's role model, his father so long a part of the past that he was not remembered.

Years later, Leigh recalled Uncle Boots with amusement. "He was a little guy, five foot seven, with a full head of hair, dark brown, and dark skin. He looked like an Indian, or a hobo down on his luck." Boots would sometimes sleep off a drunk in the back seat of his car, Leigh said.

"One time when he was sleeping, drunk, in the back seat, the car was stolen," Leigh said. "Boots woke up and started fighting with the guy who stole it, and he was still behind the wheel. I mean the car was moving! It was right in the middle of Reading Road," Leigh said, referring to a Cincinnati main street.

Boots died of cancer "sometime during the past ten years," Leigh said. "Seems like most everyone in my family dies of cancer."

The Helpers

With the investigation in progress, police got phone calls, some anonymous, about sightings of people with beards (John Leigh had a fragile fringe running from ear to ear under his chin), about people acting suspiciously, about people with names similar to those sought. Everyone wanted to get into the act. All calls were recorded and checked out. It was time consuming, not much help and sometimes funny. There also were law enforcement queries from numerous jurisdictions.

- There was a report of a June 5 holdup of a Gatliff, Kentucky restaurant in which "the big man had to hold down the smaller, excitable man who wanted to kill the people in the restaurant." While it was true that of the men sought in the Delhi crime one was quite big and the other smaller, neither of the guns reported stolen from the Kentucky restaurant was involved in the Cabinet Supreme holdup.
- One call came from a building and loan clerk in another Cincinnati suburb, who said a man with a beard deposited $370 on September 24. She said the man was on probation in another county. Aside from the fact that it was unlikely that a robber would take money from one bank and stash it in another the same day, the amount taken in Delhi was $275.
- A lead on a license plate was erroneous, but turned out to belong to a man known to Cincinnati District Five police for minor offenses. Somebody didn't like him, and made the phone call.
- A man was picked up by police near 13th and Vine in the city on the day of the robbery because he was about the right height of one of the

suspects who had red hair, but this guy had a red beard. He was released. The wanted man was clean-shaven.

- One curious call came from a Milwaukee banker who on the day of the murders happened to be in a Cincinnati restaurant at the same time as two white males, one of whom had a beard. The banker reported the man with the beard said they knew about the Delhi holdup and when asked, said yes, they did it, and left the restaurant. Oddly, the banker first returned to Milwaukee where he called the local FBI office which in turn notified Cincinnati FBI. It led to nothing.

- A man called to say he saw three men fitting the descriptions (they didn't) of the wanted men. "He further states he personally solved a murder four years ago for (Hamilton County Sheriff) Dan Tehan," the doubting officer reported.

- There was the service station owner in the tiny Ohio River town of Cleves, calling to say that a potato chip driver-salesman told him he saw three men who looked like the wanted men in a local cafe. The officer who took the report drove to Cleves, where he discovered that the "suspects" were three local residents whom he knew, none of whom matched the wanted descriptions.

Inquiries from a variety of law enforcement officials asked for more information because of possible sightings of the fugitives, or as possibly related to crimes in their areas. Those queries came from Alabama, Florida, Indiana, Kentucky, Missouri and elsewhere in Ohio.

A lot of people were paying attention.

Chapter Seven

Kassow's Tale

Raymond Kassow became increasingly tense and nervous as investigators resumed questioning him. During initial interrogation at Delhi police headquarters and the polygraph exam he steadfastly denied knowledge of the crime.

The twenty-four-year-old had been arrested without resistance at his Denver Street home, about five houses away from the residence of victims Henrietta and Luella Stitzel. He was taken into custody within three hours of the holdup.

5:30 pm, Thursday

While Chief Makin spoke with the parents of Watterson Johnson in an effort to determine the whereabouts of their son, Kassow was questioned again, by Sergeants Russell Jackson and Eugene Moore at the crime bureau. The purpose of the continuing interview was to determine whether to place charges against Kassow or to release him.

Kassow was visited at the crime bureau by his older brother, Ellis, whom he asked to see. After the brothers talked privately, Makin joined Jackson and Moore when they returned to the interview room where the brothers waited.

The cumulative effect of almost thirty hours in police custody, constant questioning and the fraternal visit was to loosen Kassow's tongue. He was agitated and asked for a waste basket, into which he promptly threw up. Then he started to talk.

"I wouldn't be in this mess if it weren't for Carl Ingle," Kassow began. Ingle was Jerry Grueter's handyman, who did repair on the manager's rental property, as well as on some savings and loan property.

Kassow said Ingle approached him about robbing the savings and loan, telling him a lot of money was kept there. "I told Ingle I didn't want any part of it," Kassow said, but Ingle persisted. Later, Ingle talked to Watterson Johnson to see if he was interested, Kassow said, and finally, Johnson and Kassow both listened.

Johnson brought John Leigh into the scheme, Kassow told police. He admitted driving the getaway car, but denied entering the building, denied killing anyone and denied having a gun. He said Leigh and Johnson went into the building and when they came out and got back in the car, they laid their guns on the console. Kassow said a lot of other things, finally agreeing to speak to a tape recorder for a formal statement.

Before making the recorded statement, Kassow offered to show officers where the guns were. He said there were two guns involved and he had buried them.

Investigators were eager to take Kassow up on his offer to retrieve the guns, but they had a media problem. Kassow was easily spooked, the situation was pretty tentative, and they did not want reporters tagging along at that point. Yet there they were, in the crime bureau building where Kassow was being questioned, waiting for a word. Makin arranged to give them that word as a diversion.

Detective Tom Oberschmidt was sent out to speak to the press. He announced that Chief Makin would hold a press conference near city hall in five minutes. Reporters scrambled. While Makin and Oberschmidt went to the press conference site, four investigators and the two Kassow brothers left by another door to drive to Clifton, one of Cincinnati's hilltop neighborhoods.

To the press Makin announced, "This evening I am going to sign three warrants for four counts of first degree murder on Raymond Kassow, Watterson Johnson and John Leigh." After some questions, the press departed to file the story, and Makin and Oberschmidt left to join the safari to Clifton.

Like Rome, Cincinnati is built on seven hills, and in fact, on one hilltop there is a statue of Romulus and Remus as infants, being nurtured by their shewolf foster mother, a gift from the City of Rome.

The hill on which Clifton sits is home to the University of Cincinnati, plus high and low income housing. Also in the lower reaches of Clifton is Fairview Park and that is where Ray Kassow directed his police escorts.

At the park, the eight men walked up a path to a wooded area, following instructions from Kassow who pointed to a fallen log. Police first took multi-angled photographs of the area, then started to dig under the log. They dug up a brown paper bag.

Inside the bag were three guns, one of the detectives announced. At this, Kassow became visibly upset. He exclaimed, "There can only be two guns there!" As the men walked back to their cars with the bag, Kassow asked, "How many guns are in the bag?" Sergeant Jackson responded, "Three." Kassow's upset grew extreme, and he turned and threw up. Three guns skewed Kassow's story. In his effort to convince the cops that he had been unarmed Kassow managed to deceive himself. He had forgotten what he had buried.

The weapons in the paper bag were a .25 caliber automatic, jammed with an empty shell; a .22 caliber revolver, fully loaded, and another .22 caliber revolver containing four bullets and two empty shells.

Also in the bag was a lady's turquoise billfold, carrying identification, including driver's license, for Luella Stitzel. A box of .22 caliber shells and a handful of coins were also in the bag.

Back at the crime bureau, Ellis Kassow brought his brother a cup of water and with Ellis present, Ray was ready to speak for the record.

8:10 pm, Thursday

Sergeant Moore began, "Raymond, you know we are making a recording of this statement? You know you are under arrest and will be charged with homicide, murder in the first degree, with reference to the Cabinet Supreme holdup yesterday morning? Do you understand that?"

Kassow responded *yes* to all three questions. Moore read the Miranda warnings, and they got down to the nitty-gritty.

It was not the most coherent statement in the world, but it told a story. In trying to describe what happened, self-protection was foremost in Kassow's mind. Despite earlier informal dialogue, police had trouble getting him started for the tape.

Sergeant Moore said, "In this holdup four women were killed. You were present and involved in this situation. Is that correct?"

"Uh—"

Moore tried again. "My question is you know what occurred there and you were involved in the holdup?" That wasn't the way Ray wanted to tell it. He did not respond.

Moore cajoled, "You've told us certain things about this, Ray, and that is all we want you to do now, tell us . . . what you told us before."

"I was there," Kassow finally said, "but I—uh—didn't—uh—I didn't go in the place, or I mean I didn't shoot nobody."

Q. Will you state exactly what occurred? Start any place you like, but how about who were the people who were involved?

A. Uh—Watterson Johnson and Johnny Leigh.

Q. All right. When did you meet these fellows yesterday morning?

A. Yesterday morning, after eight o'clock in the morning—uh—drove around.

Q. Well, would you like to start how this all began? You've been discussing this with Johnson and Leigh in recent days or weeks?

A. Yes.

Q. All right. Will you tell us in your own words just how this came about?

Kassow couldn't figure out how to answer a non-specific question. He didn't respond. Moore, an old hand, understood. He tried a different approach.

Q. How long have you known Johnson?

A. Since about December.

Q. What year?

A. Of last year.

Q. 1968?

A. Yes.

The truth was that Kassow and Johnson knew each other in boyhood. Each had been committed to Boys Industrial School as a juvenile offender.

Q. How long have you known Johnny Leigh?

A. For about a month.

Q. All right. When was this holdup first discussed among the three of you?

A. In the past week.

Q. All right. Do you want to take it from there?

A. Well—uh—we discussed it, and Tuesday or Wednesday morning we went out there and pulled up in the driveway and parked the car there, and I sit in the car and they went in the building and loan and what happened in there I don't know. They come out and jumped in the car and we left.

Q. Well, you knew they went in to hold up the place?

A. Yes.

Q. All right. When they came out, what did they have with them?

A. When they came out they had a purse in their hands and they climbed in the car and we left.

Q. What was said? What conversation was there?

A. That I couldn't say. It all happened so fast. That's all I did, was just left. I got out of there fast, you know.

Q. Well, you had some recollection before, about some conversation.
A. Well, they talked.
Q. Is there some mention of the killing or the shootings?
A. They said, "I had to kill her. I had to kill her."
Q. Who said that?
A. Uh—Watterson said that and Johnny Leigh said that. They both mentioned that at different times.

Kassow said Johnson mentioned it before they left Delhi Pike, and Leigh mentioned it while they were driving down Anderson Ferry Road. It became apparent, later, that who said what depended upon who was telling the tale.

Q. What did you do prior to the holdup? Why don't you give us an account of just what your actions were from the time you met, and where you met, and what kind of a car and whose car you were in yesterday?
A. Well, we met underneath the Sixth Street viaduct. The '64 Malibu Chevrolet.
Q. Whose car was that?
A. I don't know the man's name that the car belonged to. He's a colored man, is all I know. I don't even know who he is.
Q. Who borrowed the car?
A. Johnny borrows the car all the time.
Q. This is the car that Johnny Leigh uses?
A. Right.
Q. Did you have a time to meet there? Had this been set the evening before or sometime?
A. Not exactly. We generally—that's—uh—if we wanted to fool around or something we met under the bridge.

Kassow said he was under the bridge about seven-thirty or quarter to eight, but the other two had not yet shown. He left, then went back, "and they came. We sat there and we talked, and so I took my car up to Storrs Street and I parked my car. Then I got in their car and we went down River Road and wound up on Delhi."

Kassow offered a convoluted version of the route taken, which ended with the car parked in the Kroger grocery store lot. That store was just back of Cabinet Supreme, but its parking lot extended south to Delhi Pike, between the savings and loan and the adjacent short order restaurant, Frisch's.

Police wanted to know why they parked in the Kroger lot.

Q. Was this an observation? Were you looking at the building and loan?
A. Yes.

Q. What was the plan of action then?

A. Well—

Q. Where did you get the idea? When did this start and how did it start?

A. The whole thing actually started right there in the Kroger's parking lot.

That was not the answer investigators were looking for. They reminded Kassow of a statement he made previously, before the taping session.

Q. You indicated to us that there was some talk about holding up the savings and loan some days or weeks prior?

A. Before that, another man . . . told us about it and told me about it. Told me there was a lot of money in this. So—uh—later on I told him I didn't want nothing to do with it. And he started talking to Watterson Johnson.

Q. And this led up then—

A. It led up to—uh—he got hold of Johnny Leigh. So then they done it themselves. I mean, uh—

Q. Then the three of you ended up yesterday morning?

A. Right. Ended up in the parking lot of the building and loan. I was in the car. They got out of the car and they went into the building and loan. They came out of the building and loan and they had—

Q. Well, what was the conversation just prior to going in? What were the plans mentioned, or how it was going to be handled?

A. Well, I was going to drive the car into the parking lot and stop. They was going to get out. They got out. They didn't say nothing about killing nobody or nothing like that. And—uh—any mention of killing anybody I would have never went in that. Never would have went in the driveway.

Others would tell a different story.

Q. While they were in the building and loan did you observe anything else?

A. A man's car was sitting in front of me and there was a man in it. [Joe Huebner.] A woman got out of it and she went in the building and loan. There was another car—

Q. Did that car pull up after you pulled in?

A. Yes.

Q. All right. And a man and a woman drove up?

A. Right. And then the woman got out and the man stayed in the car. There was another car pulling up on the other side of me, on the left hand side of me. One or two women [the Stitzel sisters-in-law] got out of that car and went in. And then seconds later [Leigh and Johnson] come running out of the loan company and jumped into the car and we left.

Kassow related that from Delhi Pike they drove south down Anderson Ferry to River Road, back to the Sixth Street viaduct where he got out of the convertible and went back to his own car. He said Leigh and Johnson were going to the Mill Creek to get rid of the purses.

Q. Now you took us down to a point and showed us where—
A. The purses would be.
Q. The purses would have been thrown.
A. I wasn't sure. I mean they told me they were going to throw them in the Mill Creek.
Q. Who kept the guns at this point?
A. I had the guns in a bag.
Q. Did you keep the guns with you?
A. Yes, and left there. And then I went to Fairview Park.
Q. Did you go there alone or did they meet you?
A. I went there alone. They went downtown.
Q. Did you intend to meet them downtown?
A. Well, I didn't know what I was going to do. I was just shocked at everything—everything that all happened about it.
Q. Now you've taken us to Fairview Park?
A. Fairview Park where the guns was.
Q. Who did the guns belong to?
A. To—uh—Watterson. Well, I don't know. I mean if they was both Watterson's or if Johnny's or one was which or what.
Q. There were three guns?
A. Three. I don't know about the third one. I just know about the two. I don't know about the third.
Q. Why did you end up with the guns and they pick up the purses? Was there an agreement of some sort there?
A. No, no agreement. I just took the bag with me and I just—no reason. I just did.
Q. Describe what you did with the guns.
A. Took the bag and drove to Fairview Park and I went up in the woods and buried the sack with the guns in it.
Q. Was this a location you were familiar with? Had you been in that area before?
A. Yeah. I mean, I know about the park and I've been up through there. I didn't have no idea where I was going to put the bag. I didn't know what I was going to do.

Kassow said after burying the guns, he drove back down town, parked his car and walked around.

"I just met them at the White Castle, at Liberty and Vine." He said the other two went to a clothing store above the Empire Theater, then went into the movie theater.

"I was coming around the corner and I seen them going in the show. I crossed the street and give the woman in the show window a dollar. I said I'm going in to look for somebody. So I went in and I seen them two in there together."

Q. This is Leigh and Johnson?

Kassow confirmed he was still talking about Leigh and Johnson. Then, he said, "I turned around and left. And I went up and walked around a little bit and got my car and left. I went to the unemployment office and I was in there for a matter of fifteen minutes. I made a phone call. I called my wife and she said the police was looking for me." He then went to the F.H. Lawson Company to apply for a job, then went home. "When I got home I went upstairs and she wanted to know why the police was looking for me. So I went down to the garage. I said, well, I'll just stay down here and fool around and I'll wait for them. So the police came there and I went up with them."

What Kassow left out of the narration of his activities prior to arrest was that he went to his bank at the corner of Eighth and State to withdraw $600 from his savings account. Ironically, that was much more than the amount stolen from Cabinet Supreme. He took the money out of the bank to give to his wife, Betty, he later explained. He figured he would be arrested, and didn't think his wife could access the account since it was in his name only.

Before the formal statement ended, he was asked:

Q. You mentioned before that somebody that worked at the building and loan or something tried to get you interested in a holdup of the place, even before these other two men were involved?
A. Right.
Q. Now who is this man?
A. Carl Ingle.
Q. Carl Ingle. Do you know Carl Ingle very well?
A. Yes.

The session was over at 8:30 p.m. Ellis left to get some food for Ray, and Chief Makin notified the sheriff's office that he had signed first degree homicide warrants on Kassow, Johnson and Leigh. Kassow was returned to the city lock-up.

With reason to believe state lines had been crossed, the FBI was asked to issue UFAP warrants (Unlawful Flight to Avoid Prosecution) on Johnson and

Leigh. Warrant information would go into the NCIC (National Crime Information Center), data from which is available to police agencies throughout the country. At Makin's request, the sheriff agreed to pursue the UFAP warrants, since the chief expected to be tied up at the crime bureau during questioning of Carl Ingle, who had been implicated by Kassow's statement.

The Second Arrest

11:30 pm, Thursday

Detective Harry Hillman of the Cincinnati Homicide Squad went to the Lower Price Hill apartment of Carl Ingle, accompanied by six other officers, three from Cincinnati and three from Hamilton County.

They were admitted by the two youngest sons of Ingle, who was lying on the couch, watching television. Ingle readily accompanied the officers—who's going to argue with seven cops?—to the homicide bureau where he was questioned about the robbery and murders.

Ingle easily admitted knowing Ray Kassow for about twenty years. He said they knew each other from boyhood. He also knew Jerry Grueter, manager of Cabinet Supreme, because he worked for Grueter as caretaker and maintenance man for a number of buildings which Grueter owned.

Asked outright if he had set up the robbery, Ingle denied it. Lengthy questioning elicited unwavering denial. He also denied knowing Johnson or Leigh.

12:30 am, Friday, September 26

While Ingle was being questioned, Hillman went to the Central Station jail and picked up Kassow for a confrontation with the handyman. Waiting for Kassow, Ingle reiterated to Chief Makin that he had known Ray from the time they were kids, then added he "did know Watterson Johnson, that Johnson, too, had lived in the area some time back." This was a contradiction of one of his earlier denials. Still, the thirty-one-year-old Ingle continued to deny participation in the holdup, saying he "thought very highly of Mr. Grueter," that their relationship was "more along the lines of father-son, as compared with employer-employee relationship."

Kassow and Ingle were brought face to face, and Kassow repeated his story, that Ingle had set up the robbery. Twice he turned Ingle down, Kassow said. The third time, when he visited Ingle's home with Watterson Johnson, Johnson agreed to hold up the savings and loan, Kassow said. In the presence of Ingle and five police investigators, Kassow said Ingle told him "there was a lot of money to be had."

Ingle listened quietly to Kassow's statement, then said, "I don't know why Ray is doing this. I don't know anything about it."

Kassow was returned to his jail cell. Ingle started talking to Lieutenant Vogel, telling him that he did, after all, remember a red-haired man who might have been Johnson, that he (Ingle) may have been used by Kassow and Johnson because they questioned him about the layout of Cabinet Supreme and the amount of money usually kept there.

In fact, Ingle said, they had talked him into drawing some kind of a sketch. He now realized, Ingle told the officer, that the sketch may have been a floor plan for them.

Shortly after 9 a.m. Friday, Ingle was charged on four counts of first degree murder. He was locked up in the city jail. On Monday, September 29, Ingle was bound over to the grand jury and held without bond.

Jerome Grueter

Jerry Grueter, manager and secretary of Cabinet Supreme Savings and Loan, owned more than a dozen rental properties on four streets in the Lower Price Hill area. He told police, "Ingle has been working for me for fourteen years, since he was seventeen-years old."

Ingle started with him at $20 per week, with nine buildings to maintain, Grueter said. "He didn't know anything about maintenance when he started, but he got to the point where he was fairly good at plumbing and electrical work," Grueter said. In 1969 Ingle was earning $50 cash per week, but "in so much that his withholding, social security and utilities were paid in full, it averages out to between $75 and $80 per week."

The businessman said, "I advised Ingle to become either an apprentice plumber or electrician because I thought he could do much better for himself." Grueter said Ingle also did side jobs for others. He said Ingle left his employ one time about ten months before, to work for either the city or the county, but that didn't last long, and Ingle came back.

Grueter told police Ingle's work was satisfactory until about two years back, but since then he became dissatisfied with Ingle's production. He said about that time he cut Ingle's credit off because he thought the bills were much too high for the work being done.

"I told Carl in May of 1968 that he would have to start producing more work. I had mentioned to a number of tenants that I'd get another maintenance man if I could find one," Grueter told police. "I would imagine that the word got back to Carl."

Grueter added he had a misunderstanding with Ingle about two years back over a piece of property on Neave Street which Ingle wanted to purchase, and Grueter was willing to sell to him, but they had a difference of opinion about price. Grueter said while he was willing to sell the property to Ingle for the market price of $6,000, that Ingle felt Grueter should let him have it for $4,000.

Grueter gave all this information to Delhi Officer John Eschenbach and Sgt. Harry Bode, a nine-year veteran detective with the sheriff's department, on September 27, three days after the hold-up.

The savings and loan manager told the officers he felt Ingle had improved in his performance, especially in the past three weeks. Nevertheless, before the matter was ended in the courts, Grueter fired Ingle.

Chapter Eight

On the Run

Afternoon Wednesday, September 24

Watterson Johnson and John Leigh got out of Uncle Boots' old blue Dodge near the Greyhound bus station in Lexington, Kentucky, one hundred miles south of Cincinnati. John had already gassed up the car, and now paid Uncle Boots for his trouble. How much he paid is an open question, depending upon who did the telling. Boots said it was four bucks. Leigh said it was a lot more. He speculated that maybe Boots didn't want police to know his nephew was carrying much cash.

Boots went back to Cincinnati; the other two went into the bus terminal. For $4.65 each, they rode the bus south to Pine Knot, home of Rita Leigh's grandmother and her aunt, where they visited briefly. Then the aunt drove them to a Whitley City motel a few miles away, where they spent the night.

The next morning, John called his grandmother's house in Cincinnati and spoke to Uncle Boots. He asked Boots to bring Rita and his clothes to Pine Knot. Boots and Rita arrived in Pine Knot Thursday afternoon, but Johnson and Leigh were gone. Local media coverage of the murder story spooked the fugitives, so they didn't linger.

They hit the road, using their thumbs for transportation. They were picked up by a number of friendly innocents who had no idea the hitchhikers they were helping were wanted for murder.

"You wouldn't believe some of the people who will pick up hitchers," Leigh wrote years later. "It would have been easy to take someone's car that picked us up. Never gave it another thought, why we didn't take someone's car." He mused, "Wonder why? Had nothing to lose," but added, "I'm glad no one else got hurt when we were on the run." That was the retrospective of a middle-aged man. As a twenty-year-old fugitive from the law, it simply did not occur to him to hijack one of the vehicles. The people who gave rides to the two men never knew how lucky they were.

In a series of short hops, the two hitched as far as Nashville. Their first ride came from a couple of drunks in a pickup truck who drove them across the state line into Tennessee. The next helpful motorist was a teenage boy who took them a little further, then dropped them off.

An elderly couple in an old Pontiac carried them a short distance, followed by another teenager with whom they rode for about forty-five minutes, as far as a service station. An old man in a compact car gave them a ride for about eight miles, then let them out as he turned off the highway. From there, the ride came from a slightly drunken soldier who drove them as far as Nashville, where a woman gave them a ride to about twenty-five miles southwest of town. And it was there they met the Illustrated Man.

David Earl Randall

Earl Randall drove his fourteen-year-old black Ford with the Mississippi tags out of Nashville in a state of funk. He was twenty-seven-years old, almost stone broke and he missed Zonia Ophelia, his wife, who was on the other side of the country. All he could think to do was go see his folks in Mississippi, hoping his cash and car would last until he got there. Fate and the fugitives changed his plans.

"I met these two guys when they were hitchhiking about twenty-five miles southwest of Nashville," Earl Randall said. "It was nine o'clock at night on Thursday." The men from Cincinnati had been on the run since about noon Wednesday.

When Randall stopped and picked up Johnson and Leigh, the three men didn't bother to exchange biographies. Maybe that was because Randall's most recent address had been care of the Nashville chief of police, and he had done a stint at Nashville State Penitentiary for writing checks he shouldn't have written. And the fugitives weren't about to announce their status.

Leigh and Randall had a few things in common. They were about the same height and weight, had brown hair and both were tattooed. But Randall's tattoos put Leigh's in the shade. John Leigh's tattoos were all on his left arm and hand. On the lower arm was a spider with "John" and a ribbon painted above it; further up on the arm was a heart. The letters *L O V E* were on the back of his hand, one letter on each of four fingers. The finger tattoos had been done with needle and thread when Leigh was thirteen years old, hanging out on street corners.

By comparison, Earl was the Illustrated Man. On his left arm was a naked lady. There was the word "death" with a skull and crossbones. There was the name "Sue" and a heart with a knife through it. There was an eagle with a globe. On the right arm was a devil's head and a pitchfork. And over the right bicep, a woman in a bikini. Earl missed his wife, but never said what Zonia Ophelia thought of the "Sue" tattoo, the naked lady or the bikini babe.

As Randall picked up the hitchhikers, he told them he was going to Mississippi to visit his father. But when his new friends, "Big Red" and Johnny, told him "they had enough money to pay for gas, oil and eats for the three of us all the way to California, I decided to go to Bakersfield to see my wife. They showed me $40 between them, and we took off for California. They said they wanted to go there to get jobs."

The compatible trio headed west by way of Memphis, Tennessee; Little Rock, Arkansas; Oklahoma City, Oklahoma; Amarillo, Texas and Albuquerque, New Mexico, traveling mostly on Route 66 and Interstate 40. Before they left the State of Tennessee, they picked up two more hitchhikers who stayed with them almost a little too long.

A couple of unkempt teenagers, about sixteen or seventeen, were thumbing on the highway. The three men in the Ford thought the boy and girl probably were runaways, and they decided to give the kids a lift. Both youngsters wore earrings and LOVE insignia and didn't make a whole lot of sense. Teenage hippies, the men thought. Except for the fact that the kids just plain smelled bad, they were no trouble until they got to Texas. By then, it became apparent that his companions were getting a little too interested in the girl, Leigh thought, a complication none of them needed. Besides, it was crowded with the kids in the car. The others agreed—time to get rid of them.

As they headed into Oklahoma, the old Ford's water pump gave up the ghost and the travelers sought a junk yard for an affordable replacement. They found one, and everybody got out of the car to reconnoiter for the needed part. Randall found the right pump and Leigh paid for it. The men worked on the car, installing the pump, while the kids wandered around. The pump installed, the men took off, leaving the Tennessee teenagers to shift for themselves in the Oklahoma junk yard. It was just as well, both for the girl and the fugitives.

Shortly after resuming the journey, with Leigh driving, the Ford was pulled over by the State Highway Patrol at Pryor, Oklahoma, and Leigh was asked for identification. A tail light was not working, a patrolman said. If the kids still had been in the car, the officer might have run a computer check on Leigh's identification. But he never did.

Leigh was taken into the police cruiser and was told the ticket would cost $25. He got the money from Johnson and paid the patrolman on the spot. The officer never knew he had a murder suspect in his cruiser.

"John drove quite a bit of the time while I slept," Randall said. "John drove very fast, up to ninety and one hundred miles an hour. I had to keep telling him to slow down. Red didn't drive at all."

California-bound, they continued west on I-40 through Albuquerque to about twelve miles past Gallup, New Mexico, where fatigue caught up with them. With Randall at the wheel, Johnson sitting next to him and Leigh already drowsing in the back seat, the weary travelers pulled off the road, relaxed and fell asleep.

That was about as far west as they got.

The Last Arrests

Shortly after midnight on Sunday morning, September 28, three New Mexico State policemen met for coffee. Late night restaurants were few and far between outside of Albuquerque, so they planned to leave two cruisers and all ride in the third one to a place they could get coffee, a common practice when working the late night shift.

En route to the coffee stop, the patrolmen noticed a car with Mississippi tags parked off the roadway, with its lights off. They pulled in to check, and found three men sleeping.

"We went up and tapped on the window," said New Mexico State Policeman Raymond Harkleroad. "They stepped out and we asked for identification." The two Cincinnati men showed Selective Service cards which identified them as Watterson Johnson and John Leigh. Earl Randall produced his driver's license.

Officers radioed the information to their post at Gallup, requesting an NCIC check on each. They chatted with the travelers, waiting for a response from NCIC, which didn't come. After ten minutes, the officers told the men they could go back to sleep if they wanted to, and headed east to their coffee shop.

Just a few minutes down the road, the troopers were electrified to hear the police radio announce an NCIC "hit" on John Leigh, wanted in Ohio on four counts of murder, armed robbery and an FBI fugitive warrant.

The patrol car did a quick U-turn and burned up the road getting back to where the car with the Mississippi license plates was parked. It was gone. The cruiser kept racing westward, since that was the direction in which the parked

Mississippi car had been facing. The lawmen realized they were heading into Arizona, and called back to Gallup, getting permission from their supervisor to go ahead.

Just five miles across the state line into Arizona, the New Mexico patrolmen caught up with their quarry. They pulled the car over, rousted its occupants and spread-eagled them on the highway. The New Mexico officers recalled Johnson as "very quiet" while Leigh kept protesting "we had the wrong people." They were unarmed and offered no resistance, but the officers realized they had a problem, as the three men were taken into custody.

Now there were six men, one of them a murder suspect, and only one police cruiser. Adding to their dilemma was that the officers didn't want their supervisor to know they were all riding together. They decided to have one officer take Randall in his own car, while the other two put Johnson and Leigh in the cruiser and took them back into New Mexico, to the McKinley County sheriff's office in Gallup. There they were met by the FBI.

The NCIC hit had come in only on John Leigh. In the sheriff's office, someone noticed that the big red-haired man's Selective Service identification named him as Watterson Johnson. The query to NCIC had gone out on Johnson Watterson. When the name switch was noticed, a new inquiry was made reversing first and last names. The second hit came. Johnson, too, was wanted on four counts of homicide.

The three men were booked at 1:30 a.m. Sunday, September 28, in the sheriff's department, but custody was relinquished to Special Agent Kenneth Walton of the Federal Bureau of Investigation. Arrests had been made based on the FBI unlawful flight warrant, and the bureau's agent took charge.

Randall was held on a vagrancy charge while the FBI checked him out. He told agents he had picked up the other two hitchhiking. "During the entire trip neither of these guys said anything about robbing a bank or being in any kind of trouble. I was surprised when New Mexico police arrested us."

As they drove across country, Randall said, "Red and John spent about $30 for gas, $10 to $15 for food, $8 for beer and $3 for a water pump for my car." They didn't have motel costs; all three slept in the car. Still, either those were remarkable prices even for 1969, or Earl had a flawed memory, probably both. Neither Johnson nor Randall knew about the extra $400 Johnny had in his pocket when the trip started.

Earl wasn't the brightest light on the block, having completed only the third grade. When he found work, he was employed as a farm worker or truck driver, he told police. However, as far as his record was concerned, he had done his time, two years of a three year sentence on the bad check charge. He was paroled for the third year and currently was not on anybody's wanted list. Randall was released.

2:44 am, Sunday September 28

Johnson was locked up in the felony tank at the county jail while Walton began questioning Leigh. He was joined by another federal agent, Edward Staiger, but state troopers Harkleroad, Ben Marino and Howard McClanahan, who made the arrests, were asked to leave the interview room. Walton felt too many officers might inhibit dialogue with the prisoners.

It has been said that the most frequently ignored advice is when police read a statement of rights to a suspect: "You have the right to remain silent." "Criminals confess anyway," wrote Patrick Malone, trial attorney-writer, because "silence conveys arrogance, rudeness and most of all, guilt." Malone said, in *Criminal Justice: Opposing Viewpoints*, (Greenhaven Press, 1987), "Confession rates have remained largely unchanged since Miranda," the 1966 Supreme Court *Miranda v. Arizona* ruling that police officers must inform suspects of their legal rights.

Michael Zander, writing in the *New York Times* January 27, 1986, said, "Very few suspects have the strength of mind to say nothing."

John Leigh was no exception. "Mirandized" by Agent Walton, Leigh responded freely, although at the outset his statements were mostly lies. The agent's questioning was inexorable, in an interview session which lasted more than four hours. Finally, a tired Leigh said, "Mr. Walton, I want to tell you the truth."

Leigh gave the agent a brief verbal sketch of what his day had been like on Wednesday, September 24, from the time he and his friends drove to Delhi, through the holdup and after. He admitted shooting the four women. His statement put Ray Kassow behind the wheel of the getaway car, and named Kassow as the planner, supplier of the guns, and the man who took charge of the weapons and money following the holdup. Leigh said he and Johnson disposed of the stolen pocketbooks. His statement was recorded and transcribed. At 6:59 a.m. Leigh was put in a cell, and Johnson was brought out.

7:06 am, Sunday

With Leigh's taped statement as a tool, it took less than an hour to get a taped, typed and signed confession from Watterson Johnson. When agents Walton and Staiger played the Leigh tape for Johnson, the big man reacted with "Everything happened just the way it is there; there's no more to it. That's my story." He answered a few more questions with brief replies, mostly, "Everything's true." "Right," and "I was there." He was back in his cell by 8:08 a.m. When they finished their paperwork, the FBI agents took the prisoners to Albuquerque and locked them in the city jail. While the Leigh and Johnson interviews were in progress, Ohio authorities were notified that the men they were looking for were in custody.

Chapter Nine

Journey to Judgment

About six o'clock on Sunday morning, September 28, Chief Howard Makin got a phone call at home from Harry Morgan, special agent in charge of the Cincinnati FBI office. It was good news. The fugitives from the Cabinet Supreme Savings and Loan robbery and murders had been captured in New Mexico. Morgan promised to call back as soon as he learned how matters stood on extradition.

Makin felt a sense of satisfaction, mixed with niggling questions about getting the fugitives back to Ohio. He knew he was going to New Mexico, and he knew he wanted Jackson and Bode with him. It was the *how* he was struggling with. In today's world even small cities run charge accounts with airlines and police officials carry business-related credit cards. It was different in Delhi Township in 1969. As Makin wrestled with these questions, Morgan called back. Both men had confessed and had waived extradition.

The next call astounded Makin. It was from a Cincinnati pawn broker, a man named Ben Schottenstein, whose shop was near city hall. He had heard about the arrests in New Mexico.

"Guess you're anxious to get out there and pick these guys up," Schottenstein said.

"Oh yes; we'll be working on that."

"Well you won't get anything done today because it's Sunday. You can never get anything out of the courthouse or city hall on Sunday," the pawn broker said.

"Why don't you figure out how much money you're going to need to fly out there and fly them back. When you know how much, send someone down here to pick it up. You can pay me back when you get the money from city hall or wherever."

The surprised chief said, "Mr. Schottenstein, I sure appreciate that."

"I do it all the time for the boys in homicide. I know you're anxious to get out there, as well you should be. Like I say, I do this often and I always get my money back."

Makin hardly knew what to make of the unexpected offer. He called Cincinnati Homicide. "They assured me this guy was for real," Makin said. "He did, indeed, offer this service to them quite often, and did so without any fanfare." Makin got on the phone and got the needed approval to take Cincinnati's Sergeant Russ Jackson and the county's Sergeant Harry Bode with him to Albuquerque. He sent an officer to pick up the money, and by 4 p.m. that day the police chief and two sergeants were on their way to New Mexico, arriving at Albuquerque's Sun Port airport at 9 p.m. mountain time.

7:30 am Monday

The three Ohio officers rented a car and drove to Albuquerque Police Headquarters where they interviewed John Leigh and Watterson Johnson. They drove down to a New Mexico State Police post at Grants, halfway between Albuquerque and Gallup, and talked with the three troopers who had arrested the fugitives. Then they called FBI agent Kenneth Walton who had questioned Leigh and Johnson. That resulted in an unpleasant surprise for the Cincinnati area lawmen.

Walton told them he would not be able to turn over the confession tapes. He said the tapes would be sent to FBI Headquarters in Washington from where they would be sent to Cincinnati so the FBI agent there, Harry Morgan, could present them at a press conference. *What a bullshit deal*, Makin thought. But he wasn't overly concerned. Walton didn't know it, but the Ohio cops had taped their interviews with the suspects, too.

Subsequently, Makin and company learned they had gotten somewhat more information on their tapes. More at ease with the Ohio officers, Johnson related that Carl Ingle had told him and Kassow there was a lot of money kept in the Cabinet Supreme office, that the best time for the holdup was in the morning, that there was an alarm near where the teller was.

Leigh told the Ohio officers that after they got back to where Kassow parked his car, Kassow took the bag with the guns and money. They arranged to meet at the White Castle hamburger shop at Liberty and Vine. Leigh and Johnson drove away, leaving the convertible on the lot of Queen City Chevrolet on Court Street in Cincinnati.

When the three men met again at the White Castle, Leigh told Kassow, "We want our part of the money so we can leave town. He went and got it and met us in the show [Empire Theater.] Came in the show and gave me the money, gave it all to me," Leigh said. "He said 'Split it with Red. You guys don't know me and you never heard of me. You never seen me.'"

Leigh was asked, "Did Ray keep any of the money for himself?"

"I don't know. He just gave me a handkerchief full of money." Leigh also told the Ohio officers that his Uncle Boots had given him and Johnson a ride out of town to Lexington, Kentucky. He had lied to the FBI about that portion of the run from justice, saying they had hitchhiked from Cincinnati.

Makin, Jackson and Bode met with Walton the next day. Looking at the agent, Makin couldn't help thinking that J. Edgar Hoover obviously had never seen this guy, or maybe he had, and that was why he was a detached agent in the boondocks of New Mexico. Those were the days when agents wore only white shirts, conservative ties and basic suit colors. This man really stood out, wearing a bright yellow dress shirt and lots of turquoise jewelry. *Cocky character*, Makin thought, but interesting.

Prior to his almost five years with the FBI, Walton had been a newspaper reporter and editorial writer for the Max Levine newspaper chain in Wisconsin. During his time in federal service Walton was assigned to FBI bureaus in Denver, Pittsburgh, West Virginia and Washington, D.C. Maybe it was in D.C. that his personal flair caught the director's eye. He had been in New Mexico for three years.

Walton was apologetic about the tapes. His hands were tied, he said. The agent gave a verbal rundown on the content of the taped confessions, and again apologized that he was not able to give them to the Ohio cops.

After the session with Walton, the Ohio contingent went shopping at JC Penney. One outstanding aspect of their interviews with Leigh and Johnson had been the almost suffocating stench. The prisoners had been living and sleeping in their clothes, and now they had to be taken back to Ohio on public transportation. Also, the officers wanted Johnson's clothes for possible evidentiary value. They were the same things he had been wearing at the time of the holdup.

"In the interest of saving money, Russ [Sergeant Jackson] decided to buy light blue work pants and matching shirts, much like normal prison attire," Makin said. "I told him they would stick out like sore thumbs on the airplane, but we sure as hell weren't going to buy them suits."

The next day the prisoners were told to bathe, then dress in their new clothes. Now they were less aromatic, but that didn't mean they could travel. While the prisoners were getting cleaned up at the Albuquerque City Jail, Makin took a phone call from TWA with whom they had confirmed flight reservations.

Delta, the connecting flight between Chicago and Cincinnati, was refusing to carry the cops and culprits. That was not a big problem; TWA would supply the connecting flight if the travelers were willing to fly to Dayton, about sixty miles north of Cincinnati. That was okay. They could be met at Dayton by cruisers and officers, and driven to Cincinnati. The change also would enable them to avoid a press crunch at the Greater Cincinnati Airport.

Albuquerque detectives took the three Ohio officers and their prisoners to the airport, where they learned they still had a problem. The capture had made a big splash. The local TWA manager had been reading the *Albuquerque Journal* and watching television news, and knew who they were.

"You cannot fly with those two men," the manager told Chief Makin, nodding in the direction of Johnson and Leigh.

"How in hell do you expect us to get back to Cincinnati without flying?" Makin asked.

"You could try a train, but you will not be permitted to board an aircraft here," the manager said.

In sheer desperation, Makin asked, "Are you the final authority?"

"Well, actually, that would be the flight captain, Ray Maddox." At Makin's insistence, the manager agreed to see if Captain Maddox would talk to him, "but I'm sure he will refuse to fly you with those two men."

Maddox met Makin in a small office, introduced himself and asked pleasantly, "What can I do for you?"

"Fly us to Chicago," Makin responded.

"What are these fellows wanted for?" Maddox asked.

"They killed four women in a bank robbery," Makin said. Maddox raised his eyebrows. "Sound like nice guys," he commented. "What are your plans?"

"Well, there are three of us, officers. We made reservations, so I know you have window and aisle seats opposite each other and a seat behind two of them."

Makin explained that an officer would be seated next to each prisoner, with the third officer seated right behind them. He assured the captain that they expected no problems with the prisoners. They were being tractable, and arrangements already had been made with the Chicago Police Department to meet the flight at O'Hare Airport.

"Can I see these guys?" Maddox asked.

"They're in the next office."

Makin and Maddox went into the office where Johnson and Leigh were sitting with Harry Bode and Russ Jackson. Maddox just looked at them for a few minutes, then motioned Makin into the other office.

Captain Maddox told the chief, "Here's what we're going to do. We'll board you people first. I want you sitting in front of the plane. After boarding, we'll take your weapons—unload them first—and hold them up front on the flight deck. After seating the prisoners, I want you to take the handcuffs off so the boarding passengers don't see them handcuffed. When the stewardess serves the meal, one of you can go up front with her and cut their meat. I don't want them served with a knife. When we arrive in Chicago, you will deboard the plane last. That way, you can 'cuff them again and get your weapons back before leaving the plane. Also, I would appreciate it if you don't serve them any alcohol."

The vastly relieved police chief said, "Sounds great to me. We sure appreciate it. I don't know how in hell we'd get them back otherwise."

Before leaving Albuquerque, the FBI had another surprise for Makin. They turned over the previously withheld taped confessions of Leigh and Johnson.

"Apparently, they saw that the situation could come back and bite them in the ass and they had a change of heart," Makin said. He added, "We did fully appreciate the bureau's cooperation in this case. They were very helpful and cooperative. Back then, when you got past the local level, the bureau tended to work towards being first in the public eye."

The boarding went as Captain Maddox had planned, without incident and without notice. The prisoners were peaceable, with Makin sitting next to the talkative Leigh, while across the aisle Jackson and the mostly silent Johnson sat together, with Sergeant Bode sitting behind them. During the flight, Maddox sent word he wanted to see Makin up front. Bode took his place next to Leigh, and Makin went forward where he answered the captain's questions about Chicago arrangements. There would be a connecting TWA flight to Dayton, with an hour layover at O'Hare, Makin said.

Maddox then surprised Makin by asking him to autograph one of his business cards for his son who had seen the Cabinet Supreme story on television. Makin felt honored. Maddox also said he would try to contact the TWA pilot on the connecting flight and assure him there had been no problem. The Delhi chief was grateful.

At O'Hare, Chicago police secured the entire gate area. Four of them boarded the plane, and took Leigh and Johnson off in handcuffs to a jail facility at the airport, where they were held during the layover. It was a breather for the escorting officers. They gave their weapons to Chicago police who turned them over to the TWA pilot of the connecting flight.

On the way to Dayton, Makin was surprised to see his prisoner, John Leigh, was given both a knife and fork with his meal. "Leigh was surprised, too, that he had been given a knife," Makin said. "But I wasn't concerned. It wasn't a steak knife and I didn't think Leigh was going to try to go anywhere."

Landing at Dayton without incident, the lawmen and their prisoners were met by a group of officers from Cincinnati to where they were escorted in a convoy of five police cruisers. At Cincinnati city hall, Johnson and Leigh were photographed, fingerprinted and locked up in the city jail. It was 9:30 p.m. September 30. Now there were four men in jail, all charged with the crime at Cabinet Supreme Savings and Loan.

At eight o'clock the next morning Makin, Jackson and Bode were back at the city jail. They picked up John Leigh, who had agreed to show them where he threw away the women's handbags. The foursome drove to the bottom of Plum Street, near the Ohio River. There, down a sharply inclined river bank covered with dense foliage and rubbish, Leigh said he had pitched the purses. Jackson stayed at the top of the embankment with the prisoner, while Makin and Bode went hunting among the grass and garbage.

They made two finds. One was a copy of *Maryknoll Magazine* addressed to Mrs. H. M. Stitzel, 1438 Denver Street. That was Henrietta's. The other find was Luella's flowered cloth handbag, which Leigh identified as one which he had thrown away. Neither Henrietta's nor Helen Huebner's handbags were ever found. Police speculated that scavengers found them, emptied them of leftovers and threw them in the river.

Leigh was returned to his cell, but was out again by 10:20 a.m., along with Johnson, for a lineup which included two other prisoners from Central Station Jail, and two air conditioning repairmen who happened to be working in the hallway when two more men were needed.

Viewing this motley crew were Joseph Huebner, husband of one of the victims; Ron Carr, who picked up the license plate number when he spotted Ray Kassow in the getaway car; Mrs. Barbara Anderson, area resident who saw the men in the convertible on her way from Kroger's to Frisch's, and Mrs. Peggy Hoosier, the Frisch's waitress who sold Leigh coffee and lemonade.

All four witnesses identified John Leigh. Mrs. Anderson also picked out Johnson as one of the men in the waiting convertible.

Chapter Ten

The Three-Ring Circus

Grand jury indictments charging Watterson Johnson, Raymond Kassow and John Leigh on four counts of first degree murder were handed down on October 13, nineteen days after the robbery and murders. Carl Ingle was not indicted. Hamilton County Prosecutor Melvin Rueger said the grand jury felt evidence against Ingle was insufficient. Rueger subsequently called Ingle as prosecution witness against Johnson and Kassow. The case against Johnson and Kassow would be stronger with Ingle's testimony. The public was screaming for conviction, and Rueger was determined to get it.

Carl Robert Ingle, age thirty-one, had an apartment in one of Jerry Grueter's buildings in Lower Price Hill where he lived with his second wife, Donna, and their two sons. His first wife, Sally, lived nearby with the three sons she and Carl had together. Curiously, the women were reported to be on good terms. They even vacationed together.

At the time of his arrest, Ingle was president of the Lower Price Hill Community Council, a post for which he volunteered. The choice was approved by the civic group of about twenty-five members. Ingle had been active with the council for about two years. When the city and the Cincinnati Bengals were arranging to take over Spinney Field near the Sixth Street viaduct in Lower Price Hill, Ingle was a member of the recreation committee which unsuccessfully battled city hall to preserve the field for neighborhood use. When he was arrested, his wife called an area attorney-politician in whose election campaign Ingle had worked, but the public office holder declined to represent him.

Ingle told police that at the time of the shootings he was at a local funeral home, making arrangements for the burial of a friend. Funeral home staff confirmed that Ingle was there between 11 a.m. and 11:45 a.m., when the crime was committed. After his arrest and subsequent release, Ingle was fired from his job as caretaker for property owned by Jerry Grueter. He was told to move from his Neave Street apartment, also owned by Grueter.

When the trials began in May 1970, Ingle still was president of the Lower Price Hill Community Council. He was described by supporters there as having "a real sense of obligation to the community."

Mel Rueger elected to try all three men on the single offense of the murder of Lillian Dewald. If he failed to get convictions, he could always try them for one of the other three murders. The prosecutor's game plan was to try each man in separate, but concurrent trials, which drew vehement protest from William Foster Hopkins, court-appointed lawyer for Watterson Johnson.

A well-known criminal lawyer, Hopkins was seventy-one years old at the time of the trials. He had been practicing in Ohio for half a century, and his reputation was undiminished. His autobiographical book, *Murder is My Business*, was published just three months before the trials began.

Hopkins once won a reduced verdict for a client by reading a tear-jerking Robert W. Service poem to the jury. For another client, a man who had brutalized his wife, then stabbed her to death, he won a mercy recommendation by describing to the jury in excruciating detail what death by electrocution looks and smells like. In Hamilton County and elsewhere in the state, if you were in serious trouble with the law, Foss Hopkins was the man to get if you could afford him. Johnson got him pro bono.

Hopkins decried the concurrent trials as a "three-ring circus," saying it would be impossible for his client to receive a fair trial. He said it was "childish and naive" to think that jurors would not know about the other two trials going on at the same time, that it was possible for some testimony, stricken from one trial, to drift into the other cases.

As it turned out, that was not all that drifted down courthouse corridors. At one point two of the defendants were subpoenaed out of their own trials to appear as witnesses in the first trial. Defense attorneys in the Johnson and Kassow trials were seen sitting in during portions of the Leigh trial. Evidence and photographs of evidence were rushed through the hallways from trial to trial. Many witnesses in the first trial were summoned to witness in the second and third trials.

It would be impossible, Hopkins argued, for the decision of the first jury not to affect deliberations of the other juries. Trials were set to begin one on Monday, one on Wednesday and the third on Friday. Hopkins and co-counsel

Harry Abrams asked for their jury (the Johnson trial) to be sequestered. That was denied by Judge William S. Mathews as not necessary.

Hopkins also objected to the method of jury selection, claiming that choosing jurors only from electors was a violation of his client's civil rights. Johnson was not a registered voter. (Neither were Kassow or Leigh.) Judge Mathews was not swayed by the argument. Johnson's trial would begin as scheduled, on Wednesday, May 13.

Featured in the first of the "three rings" was John Leigh whose trial before Common Pleas Judge Lyle W. Castle began Monday, May 11, less than one month before Leigh's twenty-first birthday. Leigh's plea of "not guilty by reason of insanity" was changed, before the end of the trial, to just "not guilty." While assistants were assigned to the cases against Johnson and Kassow, Chief Prosecutor Mel Rueger would litigate this one himself before a jury of eleven men and one woman in a trial which lasted just ten days.

The prosecutor called 19 witnesses, of whom eleven were law enforcement officials, including forensic experts and the coroner. First person called was Joseph Huebner, husband of one of the victims who testified to what he saw that day.

On cross examination, defense attorney Thomas Stueve tried to poke holes in Huebner's testimony about what he could see through a rearview mirror and past shrubbery in front of the savings and loan. It was seven months after the robbery and at times Huebner was confused on some details, but he was unshakable in identifying his wife's purse in the hands of one of the holdup men and about seeing John Leigh get into the convertible after coming out of the building.

John Eschenbach, first officer on the scene, described taking Polaroid pictures of the victims in the vault. Asked by the defense how he happened to be there—"This was at the beginning of a routine call?"—the five-year man in the small police department replied, "Not routine for our department, sir."

Chief Howard Makin reiterated details of September 24 and supplied information from the investigation. On cross, Stueve tried to elicit from Makin when and how he had gotten Leigh's name, but he kept asking the wrong questions. Makin was not being intransigent; he was following standard practice for testifying officers. Answer questions as asked and don't clutter up the scenario by volunteering what has not been asked.

Q. You got Leigh's name from somebody else, didn't you?
A. No, sir.
Q. You didn't dream it up, did you?
A. No, sir.
Q. Didn't you get it strictly from Mr. Kassow?
A. No, sir.
Q. Did you get it from Mr. Johnson?
A. No, sir.

Stueve gave up. If the defense query had been phrased differently, he might have learned then that Leigh was connected with the holdup by tracing the Graham Davis convertible through the license plate.

Jerome Grueter told the court that he had been secretary (and manager) at Cabinet Supreme Savings and Loan for twenty-two years, that he and Lillian Dewald were the only two persons regularly employed there. He testified that after the holdup he discovered that $111.05 was missing, that he remembered the date an account was opened in the name of Watterson Johnson "because it was my birthday, August 28."

Defense attorney Stueve asked him if he had an employee "in any capacity" named Carl Ingle. Grueter responded, "He was the maintenance man for my mother's property" and for two properties owned by the savings and loan, and he came into Cabinet Supreme "probably every three weeks."

Also testifying were:

- Graham Davis, who said he owned the convertible used in the holdup and that John Leigh had a set of keys to the car;
- Rosemary Stitzel, Henrietta's adult daughter, who identified her mother's *Maryknoll Magazine*, her Aunt Luella's handbag and the family's Christmas Club passbooks;
- Mrs. Peggy Hoosier, Frisch's waitress who identified Leigh as the man who ordered coffee and lemonade for carryout on the day of the holdup;
- Mrs. Barbara Anderson, who identified Leigh and Johnson as men she had seen in the convertible when she stopped at Frisch's after shopping at Kroger that morning;
- Ron Carr, who wrote down the license number of the convertible after seeing Kassow in it;
- Mrs. Catherine Dittman, Lillian Dewald's replacement at Cabinet Supreme after the holdup, who identified a signature card bearing the name of Watterson Johnson. Mrs. Dittman may have had some "there but for fortune" thoughts. She was teller at Cabinet Supreme before Lillian Dewald took the job, and later occasionally filled in when Lillian was on vacation.

Dr. Ben Yamaguchi, deputy county coroner, added a little show-and-tell to his description of the bullet wounds suffered by Lillian Deward. Using the back of assistant prosecutor Albert Mestemaker to illustrate location, he explained to the jury that an abrasion on the skin indicates an entrance wound. His testimony indicated Dewald could have survived two of the four gunshot wounds, but was fatally wounded by one bullet which penetrated her lung, and another which tore through her pancreas and liver.

Cincinnati Officer Dale McMillan said he spoke twice on September 24 to Graham Davis about his allegedly stolen car. The second time was at 10:30 pm when Davis called to say the car had been found on a car dealer's parking lot. McMillan didn't know it, but after abandoning the car on the lot Leigh asked his brother to tell Davis where it was. The officer said he sent a wrecker to tow it in to District Five where it was preserved for prints, pending arrival of a fingerprint expert.

That expert was Raymond Koehler, fingerprint specialist and photographer for the Cincinnati Police Division for twenty-four years. Koehler testified he lifted a print from the chrome strip just behind the glass on the wing window on the driver's side of the Malibu convertible. He identified the print as belonging to Raymond Kassow. His testimony put Kassow in the driver's seat.

Koehler was followed by a second fingerprint specialist, Willard Ballenger, a six-year man who was trained at the Ohio State Bureau of Identification. He identified Watterson Johnson's fingerprint, lifted from a piece of paper on the counter-top behind the teller's station. Sgt. Russell Jackson described his first meeting with Raymond Kassow on September 25, when Kassow gave police a taped confession. That was the same day that Kassow led him and other officers to the Fairview Park hiding place of the weapons. Jackson identified a black .22 revolver containing six live rounds, a white-handled .22 revolver with two empty chambers and four live rounds, and a black .25 automatic with no live ammunition, but containing a jammed shell casing.

Q. Sergeant, what do you mean, jammed?
A. It was in a position so that the gun could not fire. The bullet had been fired from the gun, and in ejecting the shell, it jammed.

Jackson said the first time he saw Leigh was when he and Sgt. Harry Bode went to New Mexico with Chief Makin. When Leigh gave his statement to Ohio officers in Albuquerque he said that "Ray told them to kill everybody in the place," Jackson testified. Leigh said Kassow provided the guns, and he identified pictures of the guns used in the holdup, pointing out the one he used, the sergeant said.

Leigh said Ray gave him the automatic and gave a white-handled .22 revolver to Johnson. He told the Ohio officers that he had shot all four women, then when his automatic jammed, he "grabbed Red's gun out of his hand" and shot them with it, too." The second gun jammed, also.

On cross examination, Stueve elicited from Jackson that during the trip back to Cincinnati, Leigh's demeanor was "very calm, very talkative."

Q. You have interrogated a man who is charged with quadruple murders, and he readily tells you a story implicating himself completely, and identifies guns and disregards any Constitutional rights he may have. Didn't you think that was a little—didn't that impress you?

A. I don't know if it impressed me. I can't define impressed.
Q. Did you think that was a little unusual or odd?
A. Not in my job, sir.

If Stueve was laying groundwork for the insanity defense, the sergeant wasn't having any. Stueve persevered. He got Jackson to agree that during all of his contacts with the defendant, Leigh was calm and cooperative. He concentrated on drawing a comparison of demeanor between his client and that of Johnson and Kassow, both of whom were described as nervous and frightened.

William Rathman, Cincinnati PD criminalist, had been a firearms examiner for eleven years. He described the crime scene search and findings, including three .25 caliber bullets and cartridge casings. From Dr. Yamaguchi he received two .25 caliber and two .22 caliber bullets recovered during the autopsy of Lillian Dewald. Rathman determined that all of the .25 caliber bullets came from the same automatic, that both .22 caliber bullets came from the same revolver. He matched the bullets to the guns given to him by Russ Jackson. He also matched to the same automatic a bullet taken from the body of Helen Huebner.

Also testifying were Sgt. Harry Bode, Hamilton County sheriff's detective; New Mexico State Trooper Howard McClanahan and FBI agent Kenneth Walton who said that in Leigh's first statement to him he "categorically denied participation in the holdup, but "Mr. Leigh was never recalcitrant or reluctant to talk at all." John Leigh appeared to be a compulsive communicator.

On redirect by the prosecutor, Walton said he had a Dictabelt recording of Leigh's statement. Rueger wanted to play it for the jury, then discovered his office equipment could not handle the FBI tape. At Judge Castle's insistence, Rueger's staff scurried around the county to locate a machine that could handle the recording.

After the re-cross of Walton, Judge Castle sent the jury out of the room while he and the attorneys thrashed out the admissibility of forty pieces of evidence. The prosecutor asked permission to substitute photographs of some evidence items (guns, shell fragments, etc.) because of what Foss Hopkins called the three-ring circus. The originals were needed for the other two trials while the Leigh trial was ongoing.

Defense attorney Stueve had no problems with that, but he objected to some pictures whose sole purpose, he said, was to inflame the jury. That included a picture of the four dead women in the vault. Leigh was being tried only in the death of one of the women. Stueve's objection was overruled, as was his objection to a picture of the guns, which he tied to Kassow rather than to his client. Of about thirty-odd exhibits (some were withdrawn during the approval process) Stueve was successful in keeping out only one, an almost blank banking slip which the judge ruled irrelevant.

With the evidence issues settled and a machine found which could play the FBI Dictabelt, the recording of Leigh's statement was played, over objection from the defense.

As John Leigh's recorded voice was heard narrating the shootings, tears trickled down the cheeks of the lone woman juror. With the playing of the tape, the state rested.

The jury was excused while the court heard a confused request by Stueve's co-counsel, Charles Hamilton.

Hamilton: "If it please the court, at this time the prosecution would move for dismissal of the charges."

It was a standard motion. What was not standard was defense counsel forgetting what side he was representing.

Judge: "You mean the defense, Mr. Hamilton? The defense will move?"
Hamilton: "Yes."
Judge: "You said prosecution."
Hamilton: "I'm sorry. The defense will move."

It didn't matter. The motion was overruled. It was time for the other side to be heard.

Leigh's attorneys called only five witnesses, including the defendant himself. His diminutive wife, Rita, with the manner and mode of a vulnerable teenager, made a brief appearance which seemed to have no point other than to let the jury see her. She said she and John had been married for three years, had no children, that she knew nothing about what happened at Cabinet Supreme. The prosecution declined to cross-question.

There was one character witness. William Claude Martin was youth minister at Prince of Peace (formerly Concordia) Lutheran Church on Race Street. Of John Leigh, Martin said, "He frequently participated in our youth center . . . he had a very high reputation there. He was never known as a troublemaker. He never started any trouble. He was always in good spirits. He was cooperative, never had any problem with him at all. He was always well respected by his own peer group."

Martin said John was "not a violent person at all . . . always calm, collected, very easy to get along with."

On cross, Rueger didn't mince words.

Q. You don't know anything about this crime at all, do you, sir?
A. No.

Q. Mr. Martin, would you say that somebody that shoots four people and kills them is violent or nonviolent?

A. Under most circumstances, I would say that somebody that shoots somebody would be considered violent.

There was a bit more, but that was about it for the character witness.

The next two witnesses, like Rita Leigh, were produced just for the jury to look at. They were Raymond Kassow and Watterson Johnson, on whom subpoenas were served in the courtrooms down the hall where they were on trial. Their attorneys were not happy about it.

The sheriff brought in Kassow who was asked by defense only to give his name and address. When Rueger got into a more extensive cross examination, defense attorney Hamilton objected and asked for a bench conference. After that, Judge Castle instructed the bailiff to go get Kassow's lawyers, and told Kassow he could not be compelled to testify against himself.

Kassow's attorneys, Richard Norton and Gary Schneider, showed up and talked with their client. When Kassow went back on the stand, he took the Fifth Amendment against self-incrimination on all subsequent questions and Rueger stopped trying.

Watterson Johnson was not in the courtroom when his name was called, but his lawyers, Foss Hopkins and Harry Abrams, were to protest subpoenaing their client out of his own trial. The jury was sent out of the room while the odd situation was hashed out. The judge asked Sheriff Dan Tehan if a subpoena had been served on Johnson.

Sheriff: "It has not, sir. We were going, like we usually do, to take him outside, serve him, and bring him over."

Judge: "I understand that has not been accomplished at this point?"

Sheriff: "Not yet."

Judge Castle invited comments from Hopkins or Abrams. Hopkins had plenty to say. He had been in the middle of a voir dire examination of a prospective juror when the sheriff came into the courtroom and approached his client.

"I got the idea they were asking him to step outside to be served with this subpoena issued by this court. Both Mr. Abrams and I advised our client to keep his seat and not go out. Of course the sheriff could have taken him out, that is, forcibly, but he cooperated. We feel that he [Johnson] does not have to accept this subpoena. We feel that he is in court against his will having been indicted by the Hamilton County Grand Jury, that he is on trial for murder himself and I think the mere fact of producing him in this courtroom may be in error. We have three trials going on here at once, and I think an abundance of caution should be exercised."

Leigh's lawyer, Hamilton, explained the subpoenas had been issued "to produce those two gentlemen in this courtroom for purposes of identification . . . . We feel as part of the defendant's case it is necessary for the jury to see these two gentlemen in this courtroom . . . . We feel it is very critical to our case." Hamilton said he and Stueve had talked with both judges in the other two courtrooms about the possibility of taking short recesses for "the two or four minutes" it would take to bring Kassow and Johnson into the Leigh courtroom.

He said, "We do not intend to interrogate (them) without counsels being present or otherwise impede or prejudice their case. God knows we wouldn't do that under any circumstances. They have problems of their own."

The prosecution agreed with Hamilton's "analysis." The judge said he would see them all in chambers. When they emerged, Hopkins filed a formal motion of protest.

Noting that he and Abrams represented Johnson, Hopkins stated, "We are objecting to his appearance before Judge Castle for any purpose whatsoever and take exception to his honor's ruling in ordering his appearance." Nevertheless, it was done.

John Leigh took the stand. Within minutes, Watterson Johnson came into the courtroom accompanied by his attorneys and the sheriff. They just stood in the back of the courtroom as Leigh was asked simply to look at Johnson; then Johnson and entourage departed. The Leigh jury now had seen Kassow and Johnson, both of whom loomed large in comparison with the slightly built John Leigh.

Questioned by Hamilton, Leigh recounted the events of September 24, adding that Kassow "said something about he couldn't take his car up there [Delhi] because everybody in the neighborhood knowed it and the officer done stopped him once and asked him something about a stolen check." He told Hamilton he didn't remember the waitress at Frisch's "but she had the order right," including the lemonade.

Leigh now recanted his confessions to police. Now he placed himself in the driver's seat and Kassow inside the savings and loan. "I was just to set in the car and wait for them to come out."

He said the other two were in the building longer than anticipated, so he got out of the car and went towards the door "to see what was going on. I got about halfway towards the door and I ran into Johnson and Kassow. Kassow was hollering, 'Get the hell out of here.' That is just what I did. I ran back to the car and jumped in."

He said Kassow later explained "he had to shoot somebody because he knew them. He knew them or they knew him. I don't remember which way it went."

He said after the holdup Kassow was to get rid of the guns and told him to dump the handbags in the Mill Creek, but he couldn't find a parking place near the creek, so he "went down to the [Ohio] river and threw them on the riverbank where the officers found them."

Leigh testified that after Kassow gave him the handkerchief full of money in the theater, he "drove all over town looking for my wife, Rita because I was threatened [by Kassow] that her life may be in danger." He said the statements he gave to police in Albuquerque were not made under oath. He said he had confessed to the shootings because "I was worried about my wife."

His attorney asked him point blank, "John, did you while perpetrating a robbery purposely and intentionally kill Lillian Dewald?"

Leigh responded, "No sir, I did not."

"Have you ever killed anyone in your life?"

"No sir."

"Did you know Lillian Dewald?"

"No sir."

"Did you have any reason to wish her ill?"

"No sir."

"Did you know any of the other ladies in that building and loan?"

"No sir."

"Heard their names?"

"Only after I was arrested and brought back here and put in a cell."

"To your knowledge, did Raymond Kassow know any of those women?"

"Yes sir; he knew three of them."

Rueger questioned Leigh at length on the cross examination. Leigh admitted that he had previously been arrested "for receiving and for joy-riding" for which he had spent some time in the Cincinnati Workhouse. He said he had done work on Graham Davis's car and drove it "almost every other day, just whenever he wasn't using the car."

Q. You were going to take your wife down to the bus station before or after the holdup?

A. Not either. I lied to Graham to get the car.

Q. Did you have Graham's key to the car?

A. Yes, sir.

Q. You always carry it?

A. Had a key to his car, and to his house all the time.

Q. All the time. Well, you are living in his house part of the time, aren't you?

A. I stayed there quite a bit, yes.

Q. Even though your wife is down at your house?

A. Yes, sir.

Q. In fact, Graham gives you money, doesn't he?

A. Yes, sir; working on his car.

Q. He gives you money for not working on his car, too, doesn't he?

A. No, sir.

There were a lot more questions, mostly rehashing the events of September 24, with Leigh insisting he had not gone into the savings and loan. Rueger questioned him about money, after Leigh described Kassow handing him a "handkerchief full of money."

Q. This is the money you spent when you left town?
A. Some of it.
Q. You had some when you were arrested, didn't you?
A. I had some fifty dollars when I was arrested.
Q. Still had that much left?
A. Yes, sir.

Leigh did not volunteer the information that when he and Johnson ran from Cincinnati, in addition to whatever was in the "handkerchief full of money" handed to him by Kassow, he had four hundred dollars in his pocket, taken in a burglary before the holdup.

Rueger persisted in detailed cross-questioning, and Leigh stuck to his revised version. Rueger finally tired of the game and the court quit for the night.

The next morning, Tuesday, May 19, defense attorney Stueve first reiterated all of his previous objections (laying groundwork for appeal), then withdrew the written plea of "not guilty by reason of insanity. We have offered no evidence on that subject, and we intend to offer no evidence on that subject." The court accepted the changed plea, and the defense rested.

While it was never explained, the plea change may have been related to a court-ordered psychiatric examination, done at the request of the defense. A panel of three psychiatrists interviewed Leigh separately, then pooled their findings which were not helpful to the defense.

"Mr. Leigh was cooperative with all examiners, spoke readily, showed no hesitation in revealing himself." He was not pressed for details of the crime. Emphasis was on his mental capacity, ability to assist his attorney in his defense, and potential presence of active mental disease.

Leigh painted a lurid picture of himself as he tried to make an impression on the psychiatrists. He told them he had problems with the law since he was six or seven years old. "He also claims that he has been arrested a number of times and been in the city jail on five different occasions." He said while he had been married for the past three years, he had not worked, but "supported himself by living off homosexuals for the past two years." Yet . . . "he claims he is able to have normal heterosexual relations with his wife. He denies being a homosexual himself, but claims that he does this only as a means of support." Leigh told them he had . . . "relations with other women before he met his wife and has never had any particular difficulty with this."

Leigh described himself as a heavy drinker. He also told the psychiatrists that "he has been hearing voices and seeing things ever since age eleven when he was hit on the head with a baseball bat." But the report noted that Leigh "shows no clinical evidence of auditory or visual hallucinations."

He told the doctors that ever since he was picked up by police in New Mexico . . . "he has been laughing and carrying on and joking, and claims that he has not been concerned about his predicament. However, he makes some remarks which indicate that he does know the gravity of his situation," the doctors asserted. They noted that Leigh "is very careful to make sure that the examiners understand clearly just what he is saying and what he means."

Leigh was "very oriented for time and place and person. His fund of general information appears to be slightly better than average judging from his vocabulary and his ability to handle common test phrases." That included providing abstract meanings to various proverbs. In addition, "He is able to handle serial calculations well," they said.

The report concluded that Leigh's ability to perceive his environment did not appear to be impaired, that he was not suffering from a mental disorder, that he was competent to stand trial and to assist his attorney in his defense.

There was also the fact that Leigh had calmly testified that despite his statements to both the FBI and Ohio police, he did not shoot the women, claiming he had said that he shot them only because he feared for his wife who had been threatened. If he did not shoot the women and was admitting only to participating in the holdup, there was no reason for him to plead insanity. His attorneys knew that a guilty verdict was probable. They were just trying to save their client's life.

Summing up for the prosecution, Albert Mestemaker leaned heavily on evidence from the forensic experts, quoted from Leigh's two statements to police and reminded the jury what other witnesses had said.

In closing for the defense, Charles Hamilton did not dispute most of the facts, but said there was no evidence that Leigh had entered the building or killed anyone. No fingerprint of Leigh was found inside the savings and loan. He also talked about "the bullet angles going into the bodies." He said the women were tall, that Leigh was short, that "in order to shoot somebody in the head he would have to be on a stepladder." In fact, Lillian Dewald was five feet seven, one inch shorter than Leigh, and the other three women were five feet four and under.

Hamilton admitted that when Kassow approached Leigh with the idea of the robbery . . . "the seeds were thrown on fertile and ripe ground." He hammered on Kassow as the man who was known to police in Delhi, characterizing him as "the town bully," as the planner and supplier of guns. He said "Kassow knew he had a pigeon . . . intimidating John Leigh and saying Rita is dead if you open your mouth other than to say what I am going to tell you . . . he was calm throughout all the interrogation because he knew he was going to get his moment of truth in this courtroom."

Hamilton did not seek exoneration of his client. He asked for mercy. A verdict of guilty with a recommendation of mercy would mean life in prison instead of electrocution. "We leave in your hands the question of life or death for John Leigh."

Thomas Stueve reiterated the alleged threat against Rita's life, describing Leigh as a "stooge" for Kassow and Johnson. He stressed that Kassow had reason to kill Dewald and the Stitzel women because they knew him. "When the other two ladies came in who live on the same street as Kassow—who could ever predict something like that? That is one of the most fantastic coincidences in the history of the city . . . two women walk in, of all the depositors in that bank, the two who live on Kassow's street."

The prosecutor got the last word. He lightly dismissed the testimony of the Lutheran youth minister because "church is one of the places I guess all of us are good." He reminded the jury that regardless of who did the shooting, "aiders and abettors" are equally guilty. He challenged the jury to have "the guts to do it," to bring in a guilty-as-charged verdict.

Judge Castle's charge to the jury was lengthy, amounting to twenty typewritten pages. It included instruction in the law accompanied by a list of do's and don'ts for jurors.

Juries are told to forget many things they have seen and heard. They are not told how to erase from their minds images evoked from viewing the crime scene; answers to questions which they have been told to disregard, or attorney arguments, none of which is evidence. "Don't look at that Big Pink Elephant standing in the courtroom," juries are instructed, as the elephant looms Bigger and Pinker.

Judge Castle told the jury there were four possible verdicts for them to consider: not guilty; guilty of manslaughter; guilty as charged with a mercy recommendation, or guilty of first degree murder as charged which would mandate the death penalty.

It took the Leigh jury just four-and-a-half hours, divided by dinner and an overnight in a downtown Cincinnati hotel, to return a verdict of guilty as charged. As he was led out of the courtroom, Leigh remarked to Bailiff Stanley Heber, "I'm glad it's over. I'd sooner be on Death Row than in jail here." Leigh's remark was a commentary on the quality of life during his eight months in Hamilton County Jail.

For the defendant the trial had been an unreal experience, almost like being in a movie. FBI agent Ken Walton on the witness stand looked to John Leigh just like Effrem Zimbalist Jr. and results seemed a foregone conclusion.

The trial had lasted ten days. Leigh's execution date was set for September 24, 1970, one year to the date after the quadruple murders. John Leigh would mark his twenty-first birthday, June 5, on Death Row.

When it was all over, Prosecutor Melvin Rueger said, "I have been as much concerned with the Delhi case as anyone. My wife was a personal friend of Lillian Dewald and, in fact, was to have played cards with her that night."

Chapter Eleven

In the Second Ring

If the concurrent trials were a circus, then Watterson Johnson played chief clown at his own trial. He simply refused to cooperate.

Two days after the trial opened, defense attorneys filed with the court a "Suggestion of Insanity" which stated that Johnson "is of unsound mind; that he does not understand and appreciate the nature of the charge against him, nor does he comprehend his present situation, nor is he able to assist counsel in the preparation of a defense." Judge William S. Mathews said the motion was improper because it was not accompanied by a physician's report.

As Johnson's tenuous grasp on reality became apparent during the trial, it seemed strange that his two seasoned defense attorneys did not file a request with the court, as did Leigh's lawyers, for examination by a court-appointed psychiatrist. It is possible that the client refused the service. In that case, an attorney's hands would be tied.

During presentation of the prosecution's case, which mostly mirrored the case against Leigh, Johnson denied ever having been in Cabinet Supreme Savings and Loan. He told the jury, "This false accusation has terribly offended and humiliated me."

He would not respond to questions from the prosecutor except to say, "Sir, I won't answer . . . because you people around here say I killed somebody and I didn't do it."

Whether to sequester the jury was a major battle both before the trial began on Wednesday, May 13, and later, with defense and prosecution switching stance.

The Johnson trial was in full swing when the Leigh jury brought in a verdict at 11 a.m. on Wednesday, May 20. For Johnson's defense counsel, Judge Mathews' initial refusal to sequester the jury was a sore point which erupted into a boil on the morning of May 20 when assistant prosecutor Robert Sachs asked that the jury be sequestered "from this time on."

It was clear that prosecutors knew the Leigh jury verdict was imminent and they wanted to forestall some possible events. A guilty verdict for Leigh could be basis for appeal in the Johnson case where the jury had not been shielded from news reports of the first case. A less likely possibility was that if Leigh were to be found guilty, then the Johnson jury might be reluctant to find Johnson equally culpable. The prosecution was going for a death sentence, guilty with no mercy recommendation.

Defense co-counsel Harry Abrams now objected to the prosecution asking for sequestration when it had been refused to the defense. It was too late, Abrams indicated; the news cats were out of the bag. Abrams asked the court to await comment from his co-counsel, the well-known William F. Hopkins, who had not yet arrived in the courtroom.

Judge Mathews commented, "Well now, court was to start at 9:15 a.m., and it's now 9:37 a.m." His disposition was not sweetened by the knowledge that Foss Hopkins was holding court with reporters around the corner in the pressroom.

Abrams said, "Let me get him. I'll go over and get him."

Mathews snapped, "He knows that court is to start at nine fifteen. I don't think he needs a nursemaid." All Abrams could do was to reiterate an objection to sequestering the jury at this point in the trial.

At that juncture, Hopkins strolled into the courtroom and was updated by Abrams who asked him to follow through.

Hopkins: "I'd like to hear from them what reason they have to sequester the jury now when before—and it's a matter of record—they opposed it."

Sachs: "I don't know what law requires us to explain to counsel any reason we're giving for a motion."

Judge Mathews: "I think that the motion is well taken at this time and I'm going to grant it."

Hopkins persisted. "Can I inquire of Your Honor, since the jury is not here, why this motion was not granted at the time we made it?"

The judge replied, "Because the court didn't feel it was necessary at that time . . . now the Leigh jury has not reached a verdict yet, but in all probability they will today. By sequestering this jury at this time even though those jurors have indicated that they would not be influenced by anything that happened in another courtroom, I *know* they won't be influenced if they don't know what happened."

Hopkins continued to argue, reminding the court of his previous statements, that he didn't think a non-sequestered jury would be able to avoid the publicity which "they're building up bigger and bigger in the newspapers." He previously told the judge that he "went over and heard Leigh testify" that Leigh's "testimony completely put the hat upon Kassow and upon Johnson, our client." He had said he felt there was no way that could be kept from the Johnson jury, if not sequestered. But the prosecution objection prevailed at that time, with Sachs advising the judge "You might threaten them [the jury] with the fact that you have the power to sequester them, and if there's any hint that they're not following these instructions—how you'd ever find out is, of course, impossible."

In admonishing the jury to avoid outside-the-courtroom exposure to the case, Judge Mathews touched on the problem of family discourse. "You're going to have to tell them when the case is over you can talk to them till you're blue in the face about it, if you want to do so, but for the time being you just absolutely cannot talk to anyone about the case."

All that was when the trial began on May 13. Now it was different. Hopkins queried, "Why does it make any difference because the prosecuting attorney makes the motion?" It didn't do him any good.

Judge Mathews explained that by sequestering "this jury at this time if we get moving on this case, we'll finish it today and this jury will never know what happened to the Leigh case until after they've decided this case."

Hopkins: "You mean if they're sequestered and they go out to lunch and see the headlines, they won't know?"

Judge Mathews: "You're presuming that they are going to be out to lunch."

Hopkins: "You're the one that presumed."

Judge Mathews: "I say you're presuming that they are going out to lunch. For your information, they are not going out for lunch."

Hopkins: "Well, they're not going to sleep in the courthouse. They are going out to a hotel."

Judge Mathews: "*All right.*" The argument had gone on at length and the judge had enough. "This motion to sequester the jury will be granted."

The defense team had other problems. More than once Johnson tried to fire his court-appointed attorneys who were regarded as two of the best in the business. When Johnson was on the stand, Hopkins tried to get him to repeat what Sgt. Russ Jackson said to him on the plane coming back from New Mexico, that Johnson "had a lot of life ahead of him." The implication was that Johnson need not fear a death sentence.

Q. Coming back in the airplane what did you talk about, you and the sergeant?

A. Well, there's so many things here that confuse me. Like I got on this airplane. I've never rode on an airplane in my life, and it was against my will to get on this thing now at the time, and all this stuff. I just went along with these in trying to—just felt that since I've been under their custody here that I just had to go along and do anything they said.

Q. Now I'm going to ask you again what you talked about . . . . Will you repeat what you just told Mr. Abrams and myself back there [at the table] before I put you on the stand, in reference to the conversation with Sergeant Jackson, what Sergeant Jackson may have said to you or not?

A. Sir, I don't know nothing about these killings. I haven't committed this crime. I don't even know what I'm doing here against my will, but I've been going along with this.

Hopkins relinquished the effort and the prosecution declined to cross question at that point. Later, after some forensic evidence had been discussed and admitted, Johnson indicated he wanted to make a statement. The jury was sent out of the room, and the defendant spoke.

"Well sir, now, all this has been going on, that is all hearsay, it's false and everything. All this is not true and these lawyers here they're talking about somebody giving me some guns and I had some guns and I murdered—no, this is not true. So I think these lawyers here are going along with what everybody else is saying. All this hearsay, I can't see it." For Johnson, it was quite a speech.

Abrams:　"What do you want the judge to do?"

Johnson:　"Well I want him to know how I feel here. It seems like they ain't, you know—seems like they're listening to all this hearsay and stuff that's not true and that they're not doing anything."

Hopkins responded. "Mr. Abrams and I are doing everything possible we can to defend Watterson Johnson." He said the client wanted to take the stand and so would be put on the stand "whether we feel that is right or wrong."

The judge patiently explained the facts of life in court to Johnson, assuring him he would get his chance to testify, that the jury would decide what was the truth.

Johnson continued to argue. "This ain't no justice or whatever it is." He complained about having been arrested, about the charge, about newspaper stories about him, and again, about his lawyers.

Judge Mathews remained patient. He told Johnson that he had "two of the best criminal lawyers in this part of the country who are working for you, and I don't know how I would do any differently than they are doing."

Abrams said he and Hopkins would be willing to withdraw from the case, but the judge would not permit it. Hopkins assured the judge "We are not ducking our duty here. I'm strictly for this young man no matter what he says. He couldn't say anything that could insult me. I'm here to the last ditch, and so is Mr. Abrams."

The judge said, "I don't think Mr. Johnson appreciates what you're trying to do for him." He said if the purpose of "all this" was for Johnson to replace his lawyers, the request was denied. So the matter ended.

Officer Walter Dewald was called to the stand to describe standing guard for his wife the day after Kassow and Johnson came in to open an account. He stayed in the manager's office off the lobby, he said, from where he could hear, but not see people with whom his wife spoke. He identified Watterson Johnson as one of those people, resulting in an exchange during which prosecutors got testy and Foss Hopkins got cute.

On cross examination, Hopkins asked, "How was this man dressed that you're identifying as Watterson Johnson?"

Dewald replied, "I never saw the man."

Hopkins persisted, "How was he dressed?"

The prosecution objected. "He said he didn't see him." Hopkins rebutted, "Well, he's identifying him."

An exasperated Robert Sachs said to the defense lawyer, "Do you want to testify, Mr. Hopkins?"

The unperturbed Hopkins replied, "Yes. I would be glad to." To the witness he said, "You have identified the man, haven't you?"

Cal Prem, the other prosecutor, appealed to the bench. "Judge, I'm objecting to Mr. Hopkins' conduct in front of the jury."

Judge Mathews responded, "All right. If you have any comments—and I'll say this to all counsel—direct them up here to me. Now, do you have a question on the floor, Mr. Hopkins?"

Hopkins promptly said to Dewald, "You have just identified Watterson Johnson as being in the building and loan on the 29th of August?"

A. Yes.
Q. You're now telling this jury that you did not see this person?
A. Yes.

Hopkins had made and reiterated his point. He said, "I have no further questions."

Most other witnesses at Johnson's trial had already testified during the Leigh trial, including homicide chief, Sgt. Russ Jackson, but some of the Q. and A. was different.

Jackson told the Johnson jury that he had asked Johnson "how they got the idea of pulling the job at the building and loan. He said he and Raymond Kassow had a conversation with a man named Carl Ingle, that Ingle told them there was a lot of money in the building and loan, and he described the interior of the building and loan. He also told them there might be an alarm near where the teller was," Jackson testified.

Ingle, who had been arrested and charged, but not indicted, now was called as witness for the prosecution. He testified that Kassow and Johnson had talked to him about Cabinet Supreme, asking occasional questions here and there . . . "not one question right after another of this sort; it was all assorted."

Ingle said he had drawn a picture of the layout inside the savings and loan. He explained it this way:

"I work with plasterboard because I am a maintenance man, and I draw a general diagram of the material I use before placing the material in place. So in this same instance, without thinking or without any assumption of anything I drew a general idea of what the inside of the building and loan looked like." He said he showed it to Kassow and Johnson.

That was all that was asked of Ingle. There was no cross-questioning of Ingle by defense in this trial.

Lost in a Fog

When Johnson took the stand in his own defense, he described his family as a mother who was a press operator at a Cincinnati hotel, a father who had been in Longview Hospital, a mental health facility, for "a couple of years," and four sisters, ages ranging from ages 13 to 20. The rest of Johnson's time on the stand was theater of the absurd.

To his own attorney, Johnson responded with answers to questions which had not been asked. The usually taciturn man rambled at length on his view of the case against him—"It's all false. It's against my will. There are a number of things I don't remember." He wasn't on the stand long before Hopkins turned him over to assistant prosecutor Calvin Prem for cross questioning.

Q. Johnson, when did you leave Cincinnati to go to New Mexico?
A. Well sir, this is what's been put in the paper here. They're saying that I have done something.

Q. I'm asking when you went. When did you leave?

A. Well sir, like I said, this is in the paper, and whatever you're saying and you've been saying all along here is not true. I can't believe it.

Q. I want you to tell this jury when you left Cincinnati for New Mexico.

A. Well sir, I have the right to leave, I feel, whenever I want to.

Q. Do you understand what I just asked you?

A. I haven't done what you are saying.

Q. Do you understand what I asked you?

A. Well sir, I refuse to talk to you.

Q. You're not going to answer my questions?

A. No sir, because you say I've committed some murders here, and I can't believe it.

Q. You left on the 24th of September, didn't you?

A. Sir, I've told you I can't answer your questions. I refuse to speak to you.

Q. I want you to tell this jury when you left Cincinnati.

A. Sir, I'm telling this jury that I have a right to leave whenever I want to. Don't anybody here do?

Q. You left right after you finished at the savings and loan, didn't you?

A. No sir.

Q. When did you leave?

A. I haven't committed any murders, sir.

Q. When did you and Leigh leave town?

A. I haven't committed any murders, sir.

The judge intervened. "Can you answer the question, Mr. Johnson?"

Johnson: "Sir, I'm telling the people here that I have the right to leave whenever I feel—I haven't done anything."

Judge: "Just answer the questions, Mr. Johnson."

Johnson: "Well, sir, if this man is saying that I've committed some murders, well, I can't answer this man."

Judge Mathews sent the jury out of the room and spoke to the defendant.

Judge: "Mr. Johnson, I want to tell you something. You know that your life is on the line right now. I think you do, don't you?"

Johnson: "Well sir—"

Judge: "Do you understand that if this jury doesn't recommend mercy that you're going to be sentenced to the electric chair?"

Johnson: "Well sir, I can't believe—I can't see any man going to the electric chair for whatever—charged with some killings that he didn't do."

Judge: "Well you're sure not conveying that fact to the jury, and you're not going to convey it by refusing to answer questions. If you want this jury to not send you to the electric chair, you're going to have to bare your soul to them and you're going to have to tell them everything you know about this case, and you're going to have to tell them the truth all the way down the line. One lie to that jury, and they're going to catch it, and you're going to the electric chair."

Johnson: "Well, sir, I can't talk to this man accusing me of some murders and everything else. The newspapers—

Judge: "This man is doing a job. He represents the State of Ohio. He's the lawyer for the people of the State of Ohio. He doesn't know you from a load of coal and you mean no more to him than someone else that he prosecutes. He prosecutes cases every day representing the State of Ohio, the same as Mr. Hopkins and Mr. Abrams represent you in this case . . . he has no personal animosity toward you whatsoever, and I'm just telling you now that you're going to convict yourself of this offense unless you answer the questions like your lawyers have told you to, and like you know that you should. "This jury wants to hear this story and they want to get to the truth of the matter and they aren't going to get it by you answering that you can 'leave any time you want to.' That's what we call an evasive answer."

The judge said the jury will assume the witness has something to hide, "that you're not going to tell them the truth. And right now you want the jury to believe every word you say. And now, if you want to continue on with this trial in that manner, why that is up to you, but if you'll take my advice, you'll change your attitude about the whole thing."

The judge failed to penetrate the fog. The defendant responded, "Well sir, I refuse to talk to this man. He's saying that I've committed some murders. I've set over here and listened to this, you know, and a man getting tired some time, you know, and I'm just saying that this is not true." The court tried again and again to make Johnson understand his situation, joined by the defense team.

Hopkins, Johnson's lawyer, said, "I am asking you, Watterson, as our client to answer the questions put to you by the prosecuting attorney—they have a right to ask these questions. You have a right and should give them a decent answer. That's what the judge is telling you."

Johnson: "But do I have the right to speak to him?

Hopkins: "After you answer, if you say 'I left on the 28th of September' or whatever the date is, then if you want to add something, go ahead and do it."

Judge:	"If you want to explain your answer, you can."
Hopkins:	"You're allowed to explain your answer. But answer the prosecutor's question. That's all the court is saying to you. That's all we, as counsel, are saying to you. We are for you."
Johnson:	"I can't believe all this."
Judge:	"You're not asked to believe or disbelieve it. The people that you're concerned with believing or disbelieving are these jurors."

But they were back to Square One. Johnson repeated his refrain. "Well, sir, I still refuse to talk to the man. He's saying I've committed some murders and I—

The judge wrapped it up and brought the jury back. When prosecutor Cal Prem resumed questioning, Johnson remained obdurate. The judge cut in again.

Judge:	"Johnson, you know you're on trial for the murder of Lillian Dewald in this case, don't you?"
Johnson:	"Sir, I haven't killed anyone."
Judge:	"I said you know you're on trial for that murder, don't you?"
Johnson:	"Sir, I haven't killed anyone."
Judge:	"Do you want to answer my question or do you want me to repeat it again to you?"
Johnson:	"Sir, I haven't killed anyone."

There was much, much more of the same after the prosecutor tried to resume questioning. Prem asked to have the court reporter repeat a question.

Hopkins asked, "What are going to gain by having the question again?"

Prem replied, "I want an answer to my question."

Hopkins said, "You've asked him five times. You have a way to get an answer. Why don't you ask to hold him in contempt?"

Judge:	"Do you understand the question, Mr. Johnson?"
Johnson:	"Sir, I haven't killed anyone."
Judge:	"That's not the question. The question is, do you know that you're on trial here today charged with killing Lillian Dewald?"
Johnson:	"This is what I'm saying, sir. I haven't killed anyone."
Judge:	"He hasn't asked you if you killed Lillian Dewald. He asked you if you know you're on trial for killing her."

The court's attempt to dissipate the fog appeared to have the opposite effect; it thickened. Johnson said, "I don't belong here. If I haven't killed anyone, I don't belong here."

In answer to the prosecution's several questions, Johnson, over time, repeated the same chorus with variations on the theme. His capacity for repetition was astounding.

"I couldn't be on trial for any murder."

"I'm just telling the people here that it's false, whatever is going on here."

"I'm trying to reason here. I can't talk to someone. I've been sitting over here listening to this man accuse me of some murders here."

"This is not true—these murders has got to be false—I can't believe it—this is not me—I've heard a bunch of falsation. I can't believe it."

Variations on the theme included, "I don't know what you're talking about" and "I don't remember; I was upset at the time," when the prosecutor read excerpts from his confession made at Albuquerque. Of the statement taped by the FBI, Johnson said, "I just went along with him. He told me a story."

Here and there, Johnson changed his tune enough to make flat denials of things he had said to police. He knew nothing about the guns. He knew nothing about the purses. All denials were tied to his basic point that he had never been in Cabinet Supreme and knew nothing about the place or the crime.

Court broke for dinner at 5:40 p.m. and resumed at 7 p.m. The case went to the jury at 9:39 p.m. over objection from Foss Hopkins.

He told the judge, "I think they [the jury] are completely worn out, as the court and counsel are, and I think the matter should be stopped at this moment. They should go to the hotel and have their deliberations tomorrow morning." He was overruled.

Abrams, feeling ill, asked permission to leave. Hopkins agreed to "take care of things" until 11 p.m. It was still May 20; the Leigh verdict was in, but the Johnson jury was sequestered and deliberating.

At 12:05 a.m. the jury was back in the courtroom with a question. They wanted to hear again the portion of the charge concerning aiding and abetting and about mercy. The judge obliged, and the panel went back to the jury room. Again Hopkins addressed the court about the hour. He moved that the jury be taken to a hotel for the night.

"We have been going for 15 hours and 15 minutes. This jury is exhausted. I am exhausted. I think everybody is exhausted. I don't think it's fair to anybody to have them continue to deliberate this matter. I think they should go and get a night's rest and come back here after a night's sleep and after a breakfast and finish. I don't think it's right to force this verdict."

Judge Mathews replied that he had asked the jury about that at 11 p.m. and "they indicated to me that they wished to continue deliberating." Hopkins again was overruled.

At 1:05 a.m. the jury returned a verdict of guilty as charged. Not including the one early hour morning of May 21, the Johnson trial had lasted eight days.

Later, attorney Hopkins asked for a new trial. He said that keeping the jury 15 hours on the last day of the trial made them "tired and disgusted." Judge Mathews remained unmoved.

Like Leigh, Johnson was sentenced to death in the electric chair. Like Leigh, his execution was set for September 24, first anniversary of the slayings.

Hopkins and Abrams filed an unsuccessful appeal, listing what they believed to be nine points of trial error, including the fact "that all non-registered voters were systematically excluded from jury service." Among items cited was the court's "failure to inquire into Johnson's sanity in response to a defense motion suggesting present insanity." Also specified was a protest that "the court led at least nine jurors to believe that the defendant had probably broken the law because an indictment had been returned against him." This was aftermath of a judge-attorney colloquy during the voir dire, selection of the Johnson jury.

Hopkins had inquired of a prospective juror, "You have had no jury duty before?"

"Never," the man replied.

Q. I don't suppose you understand just what an indictment is, do you?
A. Yes, I understand.
Q. What is an indictment?
A. An indictment is an accusation against someone who has probably broken the law.

Judge Mathews commented, "I think he must have gone to law school, Mr. Hopkins. That's a pretty accurate definition."

Hopkins snapped, "Well I'd have to give him a zero on that definition because he used one word, 'that has probably broken the law.' A grand jury is composed of 15 people—

"I'd say I'd have to give him an A," the judge replied. He instructed Hopkins to proceed.

"Well, I have to differ with you because I'm sure you don't want to convey to this jury that because an indictment is returned that our client has probably broken the law. That's not the law," Hopkins declared. He filed a formal exception to the judicial remarks, then went ahead with the voir dire. That was on a Friday. The following Monday morning, Judge Mathews covered his tracks. He addressed prospective jurors.

"Ladies and gentlemen, something came up last Friday that I think I should instruct you on at this point. Mr. Hopkins and I got into a little banter about an indictment. To make sure there's no misunderstanding, I think that at this time I ought to explain to you that an indictment has absolutely nothing to do with guilt. An indictment is not evidence. An indictment is merely a means provided by law for bringing the charge, that is, for accusing the defendant of the offense and bringing the matter before a jury such as we're attempting to assemble here, and the jury decides the innocence or guilt of the defendant from the evidence that comes from the witness stand plus the exhibits that are admitted in evidence."

An indictment, he continued to explain, is "absolutely no indication of guilt and should not be considered by you as such in the event you're selected to serve on this jury."

That covered the defense "exception" and apparently satisfied the appellate court. The appeal was denied and Johnson stayed on Death Row.

Chapter Twelve

The Third Trial

The first to be arrested, Raymond Kassow was the last of the three men to go to trial, starting Friday, May 15. Despite the fact that prosecutors in his case called twenty-two witnesses, three more than in either of the other two trials, it was the quickest, lasting just five days, not including an intervening weekend.

While the trials were separate, group intelligence shared among members of the prosecutor's staff was helpful in the third trial. In addition, assistant prosecutor Fred Cartolano was one of the most aggressive on Rueger's staff. He peppered defense efforts with frequent and lengthy objections throughout the trial. The prosecutor seemed to have a rabbit's foot; while the defense could seldom get an objection sustained, Cartolano seldom had one overruled.

Defense asked for a sequestered jury for duration of the trial because of media coverage of the two other trials in progress. Surprisingly, Cartolano concurred, but like the judges in the other two trials, Judge William J. Morrissey refused the request "in the absence of any showing of actual prejudice to the defendant's rights in this case."

Police and civilian witnesses who testified at the two other trials now were called to Judge Morrissey's courtroom, including Ron Carr who once again put Ray Kassow in the getaway car on the fateful day.

Carl Ingle testified for the prosecution. He said he had known Raymond Kassow all of his life.

111

"We was neighbors in growing up. He lived in one apartment which was exactly next door." Ingle said he had seen Kassow and Johnson together "twice at my home and off and on." That was in contrast to his statement during police questioning when he initially denied knowing Johnson.

He said the first time he had seen them together at his home was about two months before the holdup. He described conversations about Cabinet Supreme with Kassow and Johnson, one of which was overheard by his wives, past and present.

"My wife and ex-wife went on vacation. They had just dropped into my house" on a day that Johnson and Kassow were there. Ingle testified, "Mr. Kassow stated to me at that time, he said the Cabinet Supreme is awful small property, isn't it? I told him no, not actually, it is not. It looks small from the outside, but it is really large on the inside. At this point I drew a diagram of the building and loan."

Q. That is of the interior?
A. Yes.
Q. This was for the benefit of Mr. Kassow?
A. Yes.
Q. And Big Red?
A. Yes.

In a subsequent conversation, Ingle said, "Mr. Kassow had stated to me at that time he was going to rob the building and loan." That was about two weeks prior to the holdup, Ingle said.

Defense counsel Gary Schneider questioned Ingle about his knowledge of the savings and loan, and of manager Jerry Grueter's comings and goings during business hours. He also asked Ingle about "a piece of property that Mr. Grueter was going to give you."

Ingle said, "I was to rework the property. He was to pay me my regular salary, and by me doing this extra work he was—I myself was to pick out a piece of property. He was to sell the property to me for a reasonable amount."

Q. As a matter of fact, you did all that work you were supposed to do for Jerry Grueter, is that correct?
A. Yes.
Q. And you never got that piece of property, isn't that true?
A. Yes . . . I did not get it.

Ingle confirmed his pre-holdup conversations about Cabinet Supreme with Kassow and Johnson.

Q. And all these conversations were because of the fact that Jerry Grueter did not keep his promise to you, is that correct?

A. Yes. Could I explain the reason why that I didn't receive the property?

Q. My only question to you, sir, was that these conversations with Raymond Kassow with reference to the building and loan all transpired after Jerry Grueter did not keep his promise to you. Is that correct?

A. Yes. But it would be important for the part of the record to understand my reason.

Q. It is my understanding, sir, that on September 24 you were picked up by the Cincinnati police and held in connection with this building and loan robbery. Is that correct?

A. Yes.

And that was all. Schneider had what he wanted, testimony which might be construed to impeach the prosecution witness.

Cincinnati homicide detective Bernard Kersker, who had waded through blood collecting evidence in the vault, now described the process of swabbing Kassow's hands, part of a test to determine if he had recently fired a gun. The swabbing was done about 6 p.m. the day of the killings. Results were sent to the National Office Laboratory of the Bureau of Alcohol, Tobacco and Firearms, of the U.S. Treasury Department, Internal Revenue Service in Washington D.C. for expert examination.

Last witness for the prosecution was Maynard J. Pro, the expert from Washington, who had a notable background. He had a chemistry degree from New York University and a masters in the same field from Columbia University. He had been a research chemist for National Lead Research Laboratories, then served in the U.S. Army assigned to chemical warfare during World War II. Later, he worked on the Manhattan Project, the super-secret project which produced the atom bomb, and had been with the IRS since 1950. Pro had published about sixty articles in his field and was a frequent consultant and university lecturer.

Among his awards was one for "the technique of neutron activation analysis as it applies to crime detection." That was the method used on the sample sent to him by Cincinnati police. It was state-of-the-art forensics, an analytical system which had been in use only about ten years. Both prosecution and defense met the challenge of questioning a man who plays with a nuclear reactor by doing their homework on neutron activation analysis. Their performances were impressive.

Pro's conclusion following laboratory tests and analysis was that the swab used on Kassow's right hand indicated he had recently fired a gun. The implication was that he was the shooter in the holdup.

In final arguments, defense attorney Schneider tried to cast doubt on the testimony of the witness from Washington, noting that Pro had agreed "there are some schools of thought that don't think this method [of analysis] is particularly accurate." But testimony from a man like Maynard Pro was hard to discredit.

Probably, Schneider would have done better to have his client testify that he had, indeed, fired a gun on the morning of September 24—taking potshots at street lights. The police knew that and the other two defendants knew that.

Just three witnesses, all Kassows, were called for defense. First was Raymond's sister-in-law, Peggy, wife to Raymond's older brother, Ellis. She said Ray was just seven years old when she married Ellis, and described herself as "a second mother to Ray."

Peggy Kassow said Ray's father died when he was about five years old, and that his mother was "sickly." Mother and son were on welfare until Ray was fifteen and in the sixth grade, Peggy said.

"He was so much larger than the other children in the grade, and exceptionally large for a boy. He would come home and cry because he had to go to school with children. We used to get him off to school, then he would sneak back home because it hurt his pride."

Of Ray's work record Peggy said, he "had several good jobs, but when he would get these jobs he would have some little spats. They were minor, but then he would get a job and then something would come up. They would find out and they would ask Raymond to please quit so they wouldn't have to fire him."

She described Raymond as "wonderful" with her five boys and said "if he could have children himself he would have been a wonderful father."

Q. Do you know why Raymond can't have children?
A. No.

Cartolano didn't like the line of questioning. He told the court, "I'm sorry. I am going to object as to why he can't have children." He was sustained. Later, when Kassow was on the stand, his attorney again tried to introduce the topic, asking his client, "Can you tell us why you don't have children?" The prosecutor's interjected objection again was sustained and the matter never was explained.

Peggy Kassow continued to testify for her brother-in-law. "He would take the boys to parks and do things for them and show them recreation that my husband and I weren't able to do." She said Ray was gentle and "like a kid. He gets moody and cries and pouts for a while and then when he gets better he is back to normal."

When Kassow's twenty-one-year-old wife, Betty, took the stand, she said they had been married for five years. "He has been the most generous, kindest—"

She broke down and wept, unable to continue, and was excused. Neither of the Kassow women was cross examined.

In his own defense, Ray Kassow testified that he quit school in the sixth grade because "I was slow learning and my mother had to have income and I had to have a few things."

Q. How long were you on welfare?
A. Till I left home.
Q. And did the Welfare Department tell you that you had to leave home?
A. Well, they told me I wouldn't get any more help, and my mother that I had to get out and find a steady job.

Kassow said he had six brothers and sisters, but there wasn't much of a relationship with them. "I actually didn't really know them. I mean by the time I was old enough they was already gone." He said his brother, Ellis and his wife Peggy looked after him when he was a little boy.

He said Kassow was sent to Boys' Industrial (BIS) for burglary for about eleven months when he was about fifteen or sixteen. He said in the summer of 1969 Carl Ingle and Red Johnson were his only friends. He said he had done odd jobs for Ingle.

Questioned about Ingle, Kassow testified that during one conversation, Ingle "was asking me about robbing the building and loan . . . he said he could fix it up where it would be real easy." He said he told Ingle he "didn't want nothing to do with robbing the building and loan," that Ingle later talked about it with Watterson Johnson.

Kassow said Johnson was receptive to the idea, but that he was not. He said he had known Jerry Grueter for a long time, that his parents used to rent from Grueter. He said Johnson brought Leigh "into the picture." Finally, on September 24 all three of them met under the Sixth Street viaduct and when they got to Delhi, it was Johnson and Leigh who went into the savings and loan building.

While assistant prosecutor Cartolano did not bother with the two Kassow women when Raymond Kassow got on the stand, the prosecutor went for the jugular. Kassow having opened the door to discussion of his police record by mentioning that he was sent to BIS for burglary as a juvenile, Cartolano now reviewed other charges in his teen years: petit larceny, four times; auto theft; discharging firearms; malicious destruction of property *two* tours at BIS and almost non-stop probation in between. As an adult, Kassow was convicted of burglary and again placed on probation.

That was followed by a detailed verbal trip through the day of the robbery, with the defendant having trouble keeping track of changes in his stories from what he had said to police compared with what he was saying on the stand.

During the grueling session Cartolano pointed out the discrepancies and Kassow replied, "I don't know what I might have said about anything."

When Cartolano finished grilling the defendant, additional testimony confirmed that Kassow twice had been upset enough to vomit, once when he finally began to tell police his version of the truth about the crime, and once when he was told there were three, not two guns in the bag which was buried in the park. After that, the only thing left was summations.

The case went to the jury about 6 p.m. Wednesday, was halted for the night at 8:30 p.m. at which point the jury was finally sequestered. Deliberations resumed the next morning for about forty-five minutes. The guilty verdict came in at 10 a.m. the next day. It had taken a total of three hours and fifteen minutes to condemn the third defendant to death.

Sitting in the courtroom when the "guilty as charged" verdict was read was Raymond's wife, Betty. She sobbed openly, uncontrollably. She went home and ninety minutes later police were called to her home where she had attempted suicide. Police reported, "Mrs. Kassow was "despondent over the conviction of her husband. Took unknown amount of pills. Unconscious when police arrived." She was taken to Cincinnati General (now University) Hospital where her stomach was pumped. Because a relative reported a suicide pact between Betty and Raymond in the event he was convicted, Sgt. Russ Jackson was notified and Kassow was searched for pills. None were found.

The next day Betty was back in the courtroom to hear her husband sentenced to death. Execution was set for September 22, two days before his cohorts in crime were to go to the electric chair. All three verdicts had been returned within a twenty-three hour period.

At sentencing, Kassow said, "All I have to say is I didn't kill anybody." Johnson made a similar statement when he was sentenced. John Leigh stood mute when the judge read his sentence. All three were sent to Death Row in the (now closed) Ohio State Penitentiary in Columbus.

Chapter Thirteen

The Iceberg

They call him Iceberg. He draws pen-and-ink tattoo designs and signs his work "Ice." He paints harrowing acrylic pictures reflecting twenty-five years in the prison system. One of his most startling sketches is labeled SOCF—Southern Ohio Correctional Facility at Lucasville where an eleven day riot in April 1993 resulted in the deaths of nine inmates and one guard. Dominant in that sketch is a wild-eyed skull rampant backgrounded with graves, assorted skeletal remains and the coiled concertina wire which caps prison fences. It is Lucasville, as he sees it.

He is John Levi Leigh. At one-hundred-and-ninety pounds with a deliberately bald head and a full beard, he looks nothing like the slender mop-head who at the age of twenty was imprisoned for the murder of four women. Both arms are covered with tattoos, so many that the old Spider tattoo is obliterated. "Jailhouse skin" he calls it. He looks like a movie stereotype of the old con.

Leigh, Kassow and Johnson were not executed, nor has anyone been executed in Ohio since 1963. Death sentences were commuted in 1972 when the U.S. Supreme Court ruled Ohio's death penalty was one of many deemed unconstitutional. The state's death penalty was reinstated in 1981, but the three men convicted of the murder of Lillian Dewald at Cabinet Supreme are safe from the electric chair.

Shackled and put in a car, John Leigh was driven to the Ohio State Penitentiary which housed Death Row. Watterson Johnson was in another car.

117

At that point Leigh didn't much care about anything, but he was glad to be out of Hamilton County Jail. When they reached their destination, Leigh eyed the pre-Civil War structure (circa 1834) which has since crumbled and been razed.

"The O.P. was one big, ugly place to see for the first time," he said.

"They took the irons off us and gave us numbers," Leigh said. "The sergeant who came to take us to Death Row sure didn't look very happy about his job. He had two black eyes and his nose looked broken." The prisoners were taken across the yard to a big, black building with a steel door. The door opened, the men stepped through, and the door clanged shut behind them.

"We were like in a box now. Then a second door opened and a gate. The guards took everything we had."

The prisoners were put in small, one-man cells. "This first range was so they could keep an eye on us for a while, to make sure we didn't hurt state property, us. After about a week they moved us to another range.

"I think there was only about twenty-three of us on Death Row when I got there. There were forty-eight cells in L-Block. They used the top range for the hole—yes, we could go to the hole for anything on Death Row, just like anyone else."

Processing after arrival included physical and mental examinations and identification photos. And decontamination. "They shot us with something like Black Flag to kill bugs—thought they were trying to kill me before I got to the chair.

"We weren't allowed little things like nail clippers or a mirror. It was months before I even saw my face. Believe me, it was sure a white one. Had no sun for almost a year and wasn't eating right. No one could even write you unless they were on your visiting list. All mail was read and what they didn't want you to read they would mark out."

In each one-man cell, Leigh said, "There was a three-hole [three jacks] radio box on the wall and they would give us an earphone for one ear to listen to whatever they put on the radio. Three stations—one was black, one was hillbilly, one was for sports. It was like that all the time."

After Death Row's population had grown to about 40 inmates, Leigh said, "There was no way they could use the top range for the hole. They had to start taking us across the yard to the real hole which they didn't like at all. We would get wrote up for anything so we would end up in the hole just so we would have someone else to talk to and find out what was going on in the rest of the O.P.

"The hole wasn't anything to laugh about, but if you wanted to know something that was the place to go. If we wanted to get word to someone we knew, we would just tell someone in the hole and they would pass it on. Going to the hole was like a vacation for us on Death Row."

Later, when there were so many Death Row inmates that they were moved to another cell block, "things got better for us over there," Leigh said.

They could listen to a radio with more than three stations and find out what was going on outside. The election of a new state governor (John J. Gilligan) is remembered because "he stopped them from reading our mail and we could get mail from anyone after that. The food was better. The block was cleaner. We could get books in—art supplies in. Chess sets—everyone played it. Kept your mind off things. We could look outside and see Spring Street, people, cars—things we couldn't see in L-Block.

"You worked out all the time in your cell and did a lot of walking from wall to wall. Some guys were on Death Row a long time when I got there, ten years and longer. Got to know and talk to some people I would never have thought to talk to in my life. Very few of us are still around that was on Death Row at the O.P. when they let us off."

Escape From Death

Leigh said one day another inmate "woke me up by hitting on my wall, saying the USSC (Supreme Court) voted five to four to let us off Death Row. I thought he was talking about a baseball game. No one back then could believe it.

"Then everyone started wondering who would be the first ones to get off and how long it would take before they started. Some of us thought the guys who had been back there the longest would get off first, but that wasn't the way they did it. I guess they wanted the first ones to get off to get a lot of press. So it was a black out of Cleveland and myself." That was one black and one white, one from Ohio's northernmost city on Lake Erie and one from its most southern city, on the Ohio River.

"The news was really smoking. Johnson was still at Lima having tests run on him from going off to the nut tree once too often. Kassow got off later, about a month or two."

Leigh said, "There was fifty-six of us who got off in July 1972—don't believe there are ten of us left. I was one of the first to get off in the state at the time. They let three of us off to start with—the third was from Columbus—and the newspapers really had a lot to say about it. They didn't like it."

Former Death Row inmates were reclassified and Leigh was assigned to the yard gang "doing all kinds of odd jobs. You name it, we did it. You worked five days a week, two-hundred hours a month for $12 at the commissary and $8 in your going-home money. They stopped this about 1980. My going-home money is still there—$895.08. I can't get this money until I go home."

One day when Leigh and another man were mowing grass they saw a guard escorting Ray Kassow across the yard. Leigh stared at Kassow and bristled.

He blamed Kassow for his arrest and conviction. And he remembered Kassow saying, "If anyone goes in behind you, I'll follow and kill them."

All mouth, Kassow did nothing of the kind. Results may have been the same, but to Leigh that was not the point.

"When you got off Death Row the first place you had to go was to the bath house for a shower. A guard took you there and then to your new cell." The day Raymond Kassow was taken for his shower Leigh was working just outside the bathhouse with a friend who'd been on Death Row with him.

Leigh turned to his friend and said, "I have to go get something." He came back with a set of hedge trimmers and went to the bath house to look for Kassow.

"You could say I had something I wanted to give him. Now when you go to the bath house, you had to go down to the basement about twenty steps. I was hoping to catch him in the shower, but no luck. I opened the outer door and about fell over Kassow.

"When he saw me and saw what I had in my hand he jumped down the steps and ran out the other side of the bath house to the deputy's office. In a few days, they sent him to London" [Correctional Institution].

Prison memories washed over John Leigh. "As bad as Death Row was it was still better than the jail I just left [the Hamilton County Jail]. That place really sucked. They put Johnson and me in a two-man cell in the hall away from everyone else. Had a hole in the wall for a toilet. No hot water, a large light that stayed on all the time. Two doors about a foot apart with a hole in the inside one to put food through. Food was always cold, very little of it and full of cockroaches. Had one shower in seven months and one just before going to the courtroom. No heat in the cell. It was really cold that winter. If you didn't wash your clothes in the cold water in the sink, you wore the same stuff the whole time there.

"Couldn't get anything to read. Could have stuff to write with; think that was because they wanted to read what you wrote about. So you can see why I said I would be better off on Death Row. It *was* better."

Leigh said, "The O.P. was one big ugly place to do time, but at least you knew where you stood. You didn't ask questions. You just did what the guard told you to do. You knew what the rules were.

"Class Two Rules 1, 8 and 14 was the rules you didn't want to get wrote up for. No. 8 forbids possession of weapons or other contraband. No. 1 [insubordination] could get you an asskicking from the guards, but No. 14 [disrespect to anyone, including an inmate] could get you killed real fast. You did not disrespect another con. All a person has in here is his word. Most cons didn't even talk to each other unless it was some kind of business or someone needing something. One thing they did do at the O.P. and that was to stick together."

Death Row at the state pen may have been better than Hamilton County Jail, but there were problems. One day when John was in the shower, a guard was shaking down his cell.

"Threw my stuff all over the floor and walked on it. When I stepped in the cell and asked him why he did that, he said he didn't." The guard moved outside and closed the cell door. They argued. "He knew I was right so he didn't write me up. I told him if he opened the door I would put my foot up his ass. He didn't open the door."

Years later John ran into the same guard at Lucasville. "I told him what I thought about what he did to my stuff. He said he was sorry. I did understand he had a job to do, but he didn't have to walk on my stuff."

Leigh says he does not have trouble with blacks on the inside, but there were times. A Death Row inmate he describes as a "350 pound black pimp was giving me a hard time, running his lips about white girls. I told him no one wanted to hear that shit. He said he would see me the next walk day [when they took exercise.] I told him I would be there. I was, with a razor, but he didn't come out of his cell. A lot of guys started making fun of him after that. He wasn't big—just fat. He's dead now."

Leigh also reacted ill to "a light-skinned black that was there for raping a sixteen-year-old white girl. He stabbed her and threw her out of the car. After one visiting day he was saying things about my sister. By the time we got back to the cell block I was good and mad. I knocked him out on his feet. There were guards all over the place. The lieutenant was riding my back, telling me to stop it. Everyone had a good laugh about it. Steve was six foot two and I was only five foot eight."

Prior to imprisonment Leigh's problem was alcohol. At the state pen he added a slide into drugs.

"Started taking downers and drinking wine that was made there. Wine was easy to get—good stuff that was made at the powerhouse. [His detailed description of the potent potable made it sound more like moonshine than wine.] Ran into a pusher that got pills all the time. So they were always there."

During two years on Death Row, John learned to play chess. The condemned do not get much out-of-cell time so they devise ways to keep busy. Before they were allowed to have real chess sets they drew squares on a piece of cardboard for a playing board. Chessmen were pieces of paper on which the words pawn, rook, bishop, knight and so forth were written, or in the case of the artistic Leigh, pictures of the pieces were drawn. "Mushfaking," they call it. Improvising what you need from what is available.

As the state readied for the closing of the Ohio State Penitentiary at Columbus, Leigh was sent to SOCF (Southern Ohio Correctional Facility, otherwise known by its location: Lucasville) in February 1973.

"Got sent down there with a guy I was on Death Row with. We're still like brothers, even now. We used to work together, get drunk and high together. We were both high, or should I say low, when we went to SOCF. We went down to the cell block from receiving to see some bikers we knew—got even higher down there. Had a good time.

"That was the first place I ever did LSD. Really liked that stuff; never did anything like that before. Did a lot of it over the years." What he liked about LSD, he says, was that he "could see brick walls melting, could see faces melting." He liked the surrealistic effect. LSD is not for everyone, he says. "It's real bad news for paranoid types."

After a turbulent start, John learned there are ways to get along in the system, and ways that don't work.

"Haven't been in the hole for fighting since October 1987," he says with obvious satisfaction. "Long time! So I must be doing something right!" Because he has a wry sense of humor, he adds, "Wonder what?"

It took him a long time to learn, about seven years, he says. John may be good with numbers, but his prison history suggests it probably was more like seventeen years before he cleaned up his act.

There was a spectacularly nasty knife fight in the prison at Lucasville. There were drugs, alcohol, more fights and illicit private enterprise, all resulting in periods of solitary confinement and transfers from maximum to medium and back to maximum security institutions. He learned to hate moving day. Every time he was moved he left behind friends and everything he owned.

The Lucasville Scene

Leigh had been in the Ohio State Penitentiary for two years and nine months when he was sent to Lucasville, then Ohio's newest and toughest maximum security prison. There he promptly got involved with an inmate biker gang which had rules of its own. You had to apply to join the gang.

"Bikers has by-laws to go by," says Leigh. "No one does anything unless everyone knows what is going on."

Slights are not suffered lightly. When an inmate flashed a knife on one of the bikers, that called for retaliation. The offended man was soon to go before the parole board and hoped to go home. He didn't want to sully his record, so the newcomer volunteered. John had been on Death Row. What could they do to him? The year was 1973 and his first parole hearing in 1984 seemed like a long time away.

Leigh armed himself with "a long ice pick" crafted from parts of a cigarette rolling machine from the commissary. "They don't sell those in the commissary any more," John says reflectively.

He lurked in a cell, waiting until he saw his target coming down the range on the way back from recreation where he had been weight lifting with a buddy. As the man passed his cell, Leigh leaped out with his homemade ice pick, striking the man on the forehead between the eyes. Left quite a hole, Leigh recalls.

Leigh had not counted on the weight-lifting buddy who was right behind the target, and who carried a mushfaked weapon of his own, a sharp-honed soup ladle. The buddy lunged at Leigh and plunged the ladle-knife deep into Leigh's shoulder, hitting an artery.

Leigh put his hand over his shoulder wound and walked to the infirmary covered with blood. When the nurse said, "Where are you hurt?" he removed his hand and arterial blood spurted out, hitting the nurse.

"She was annoyed," John recalls. He got four stitches and five days in the hole, solitary confinement. He also established himself as "Iceberg" and was an accepted member of the gang.

"They brought in the Ohio State Patrol and this guy asked me how I got hurt," John related. "I told him I fell down some steps and a broken broom handle went through my shoulder." The trooper paused.

"What are you in for?" he asked.

"Multiple murder," Leigh replied. The trooper eyed him. "I guess there's no point talking to you." He walked away.

At Lucasville, Leigh says, "There was someone getting cut down just about every day. There were guns in the place. In '73 two guards got shot and killed, one by an inmate I knew. The other guy was shot by—(he named a guard.]

"Everyone was doing a lot of drugs down there. Guards would bring you anything if you had the money—pills, knives, guns. Everything was easy to get because no one really gave a shit. When the guards got shot they locked the place down and took everything we had. I went to the hole for [possession of] five dollars which I didn't have."

Inmates are not permitted to have cash. Money sent by family and friends and money earned by inmates is credited to their commissary accounts. The accounts can be used to purchase whatever the commissary has.

"They took me down the hole with nothing on and this old guard told me to take everything out of my pockets! How could I? I didn't have anything on. I was put in a cell and told to cut all my hair off my face with a razor which others had already used. All I said was 'Yes sir' and started to cut. Nothing like a good, dry shave. Only reason I was getting a hard time was because I had been on Death Row with the guy who shot the guard and because I belonged to a biker gang."

John said, "I did nothing to be put in the hole. But it wasn't the right time to run off at the mouth—two guards dead. It was 'Yes sir, No sir.' Whatever they said was right."

The paths of Leigh and Watterson Johnson converged in the Lucasville prison a few years after they first had been locked up together.

John recalled, "They called him Feet because he had big feet, size thirteen." When he was arrested, Johnson weighed two-hundred-and-ten pounds and stood six feet three inches, looking even taller because of his bushy red hair.

Leigh was shocked when he saw Johnson in 1976. He said, "If a guard didn't tell me that was him, I would never have known who he was—he looked that bad. Red was down to about one-hundred-and-fifty pounds and looked five foot nine. He was bent over and had a hump on his back and a lot of his hair was gone. He was a vegetable."

"They gave him a long stick with a nail at the end and he picks up trash in the yard. That's all he can do," Leigh said. "The boy is completely burned out. He don't even know what country he's in."

Leigh recalled when he and Johnson shared a county jail cell awaiting trial in Cincinnati that "Red kept telling me he didn't know why he was in jail—he didn't do anything. He used to talk to the walls about the trial."

Johnson "really started coming unglued when we were on Death Row up at O.P.," Leigh said. "He never came out of his cell there. We didn't get out of the cell much back then. Once a week for a one hour walk, ten minutes for a shower. Red wouldn't go out," Leigh said.

"I heard they gave him a lot of shock treatment at Lima." Lima was the State Hospital for the Criminally Insane. "Took a lot of guards to get him out of his cell. I never saw him again until that day at Lucasville."

Watterson Johnson's prison record shows that he was taken to the hospital at Lima in 1973 and again in 1978. That time Lima kept him for three years. He was moved to the Chillicothe prison in 1981 where he is currently listed as grounds keeper.

After four years at Lucasville John Leigh was ready for a transfer. Of the 1993 murderous riot there, Leigh says, "That place has always been a madhouse. What's really bad about it [the riot] is they knew it was going to happen. They just didn't know when. They're lucky more people weren't hurt. A friend of mine got killed just for trying to help a guard.

"A sad place—guards bringing in drugs, guards shot, lots of inmates cut up or killed, a woman with her head almost cut off." That victim was a young teacher whose soft-spoken and civilized manners were misconstrued by an inmate as romantic overture. He was in love. She became alarmed, but before authorities could act to remove the inmate he seized a jagged edged can lid and cut her throat.

"Glad I wasn't there when the place blew. Hope I'll never see that place again, but one never knows what tomorrow will bring."

London and Kassow

John Leigh was transferred to London Correctional, medium security. Raymond Kassow was already there. Officials knew the score and Leigh was taken to the deputy warden's office where he was warned that violence against Kassow would not be tolerated.

Leigh replied that as long as Kassow "stayed out of my face, he wouldn't have any trouble with me. But if he didn't, I would do what I had to do. The deputy asked me if I would tell Kassow that and I said yes."

Kassow was brought to the office. Leigh repeated to Kassow what he had said to the deputy.

"He understood," said Leigh. "When he left the office he was white. Don't think I saw him three times [during] almost three years. He wouldn't go any place as long as I was there. No one down there liked him.

"When I first got there guys I knew were taking bets on how long it would be before I did something to him. Guess you could say they lost. What I did to him left no marks on the body. Got into his head. Wouldn't let him go anywhere but to the commissary and to work. Needless to say, he was having a real hard time there. I knew just about everyone.

"One day I was helping Bear, a friend of mine, move his stuff to the cell block that Kassow was in. He thought I was moving in and he ran out of the block. Me and Bear had a good laugh about it.

"The commissary was in the basement [near] where I used to work in the print shop. I could see down the hall at all times. He didn't go to the commissary much. Being in that basement was a bad place to be. You could get hurt and no one would see you."

Leigh had other things to occupy his mind.

"I was into loan sharking there . . . two for one. You gave a pack [of cigarettes] to get two back. If you didn't pay, you would have visitors and you wouldn't like it. I never had anyone not pay me back. Just told them like it was."

About two-and-a-half years after Leigh arrived at London a couple of inmates came to see him and told him they were going to beat the hell out of Kassow. They said Kassow snitched on another inmate who was holding marijuana in the handle of his hairbrush. It was a courtesy visit to the "Iceberg" who had acquired a certain renown in the nine years he had been in three of Ohio's prisons. The men knew that if anything happened to Kassow Leigh would be blamed.

"Leave me out of it," Leigh told the men. "I don't want to know anything about it." Kassow was beaten, he said.

"After a while I just got sick of London—went and got some pills [speed] and let this guy see me put them in my coffee can sitting next to my locker. Didn't take long before this sergeant came up and found them. He asked if they were mine. Told him yes." That cost Leigh fifteen days in the hole and gave him a ticket back to the state penitentiary in Columbus.

Raymond Kassow stayed at London until 1984, then was transferred to the state prison at Orient, Ohio where he now works as an office porter, the man who cleans up the place.

In his second go'round at the state pen, Leigh says "I got high every day I was there. No matter where I go, there are always people that I know."

The disciplinary move to Columbus was for seventy days after which Leigh was shipped out to the prison at Marion, Ohio where he soon began to operate a thriving drug business. His official job was laundering clothes for the guards. He also used to "sell drugs by the pound," Leigh said.

"The [laundry] job was okay, but that's when I really got into moving drugs for the guards there. There has always been a lot of money [cash] in these places. I could get all the grass, coke and pills I wanted to sell. LSD was hard to come by for some reason. I knew a lot of people there from SOCF [Lucasville] and no one ever tried to take anything away from me.

"With my job I was on call twenty-four hours a day, so I could move around. I used to move the drugs up and down the halls in the guards' clothes. No one ever thought to check them out. When I took money to the guard I was dealing with, I'd put the cash in a cup of ice and head down the hall. Had a lot of guards up there who wanted to deal with me.

"There was a lot of gang stuff jumping off up there. Was always able to stay out of everything. No one likes to mess with the dope man."

Dealing at Chillicothe

After a few years "Marion started shipping everyone around to this place and that," Leigh said. He was sent to Chillicothe Correctional Institution, "the easiest place I have ever been in."

Of Chillicothe, Leigh says "I couldn't believe this place. If you wanted it you could get it—sex, drugs, anything."

He went to Chillicothe with Dawg, a biker he met at Marion. "Dawg was six foot four, weighed about two-hundred-and-sixty pounds—he sure could put the drugs away. I went to work in the butcher shop and Dawg went to school [college courses.]" Leigh also got back into the drug business.

"I was able to get any kind of drug I wanted and as much as I wanted and when I wanted it. All you had to do was to have the money. I knew enough people to put up the money before they got what they wanted. My word was gold. The person I used to get my stuff from is still working there. Some weeks I would give him up to $4,000." His contact was a food service worker, Leigh said.

The ban against an inmate having cash in his possession was not a problem for the entrepreneur. There were many ways to hide money. From the commissary one could get a jar of mayonnaise and some food items encased in plastic wrap. The plastic wrap would be removed, bills rolled up in it, and it could be heat sealed with a lighted match. The plastic-covered cash then was buried deep in the mayonnaise.

Another cache was possible because of Leigh's new pastime of making large toy wooden horses. His method of construction involved the use of dowel-shaped wooden plugs which fit into holes. Those holes could be made big enough to stash cash under the wooden plug.

An equally effective hiding place was in a can of loose tobacco, the kind used to roll your own. A false bottom was created and money placed inside. A guard checking the can would open the top and find only tobacco and some cigarette papers.

Leigh did so well he put two other dope dealers there out of business, he says. That made for bad blood and someone snitched to authorities. Leigh was disciplined twice for dealing at Chillicothe.

With the money he made selling drugs John Leigh bought extra food and arts and crafts materials. He bought a wooden bench, tools and wood. He "couldn't believe all the stuff they let us get—cutting knives, saws, drills, just about anything. Used to make a lot of toys for kids and sold them cheap—small rocking horses, toy cars. I could make just about anything I wanted to with wood." His customers were inmates and guards, buying Christmas presents for their children.

He marveled that he was allowed to have the tools, as he did about the prison job given to Red Johnson, whom he saw again at Chillicothe. For Johnson's job of "picking up cigarette butts and paper in the yard they gave him a three-foot stick with a three-inch nail in the end. Guess they'll give a nut anything."

Then he added, "I can't say too much about that," thinking of his own knife fights. "They put me in the butcher shop and gave me seven knives to cut meat with."

John commented, "Johnson was really looking bad. Don't think he knew where he was. Wonder what they had him on? You could stand next to him and he wouldn't know who you were." He described one cold, wintery day when he looked out the window in A-dorm and saw Johnson standing in the prison yard with a shovel.

"The wind was really blowing and it was cold," John said. "He stood there holding the shovel for over an hour before someone came and told him to move. He was really out of it. I couldn't believe it."

John's private enterprise kept him too busy to sample his own wares. "I wasn't really a user there. Business first. Can't think on dope—lose track of what you're doing and that's not a good thing in jail. Had a lot of heat on me because I was selling so much dope, mostly grass."

The second time someone snitched on Leigh's drug dealing he was sent back to Lucasville. "When I was rode out of there I left everything [his woodworking material and equipment] to Dawg."

Lucasville Revisited

"When I got to SOCF [Southern Ohio Correctional Facility at Lucasville] this time it was nothing like it was the first time I was there. First time, a person did what he had to do to make it. This was crazy. Nothing but head games and trouble."

"As soon as some of us got some blues to wear, they told us we were going to . . . receiving. At SOCF less than an hour and already in general population. Ran into the major [a guard] that I hadn't seen since he was a gray shirt at the O.P."

The major looked at the returnee and asked, "Well, Ice, when are you going to become an Aryan Brother?" That is a white, separatist inmate group.

Leigh replied, "Did you ever know me to need anyone to fight my fights?" The major agreed, he did not.

"I knew just about all the AB [Aryan Brothers] but they didn't have nothing for me. I was just about a loner all the time I was at SOCF this time," in vast contrast with his activities the first time he was there. John was given a porter's job in L-6 which was "mostly AB when I got there this time.

"A few months later the [inmate] clerk lost his job because of drugs, and I got it. I worked for unit staff the rest of the time I was there, all but maybe a month or two."

The clerk's job was not an easy berth. "I was almost in a fight every week because of the job. Clerks always have a hard time because you are working around The Man."

The prison had "lots of stabbings and a few killings when I was there this time, but I really didn't have any trouble. All you had to do was out-think the person you were having words with. There were a lot of kids who wanted to be killers, but didn't want to fight someone who would fight back and who knew a lot of people who ran most of the gangs."

During this second stay at SOCF in more than four years Leigh "never went to the hole for anything, and that's saying a lot." Leigh had learned a few things and cleaned up his act, he said.

Prison authorities apparently agreed. In April 1992 he was returned to London Correctional where he was carried as a low level minimum security risk. Before departing Lucasville John completed at least one substance abuse program to wean him from drugs and alcohol.

Learning at London

In the London prison John went to school and obtained a GED certificate, equivalent to a high school diploma. While working in the commissary he completed a course labeled "interpersonal counseling" which he described as "a program for violent offenders."

He said, "I really enjoyed that. We learned to walk around barriers instead of trying to bull through them the way I used to do."

John worked in the prison commissary where for more than two years he was considered a good worker, not a problem inmate. He knew he had a parole hearing coming up in August 1994.

Leigh, Kassow and Johnson had had three parole hearings since 1970. No one, least of all Leigh, was surprised when they were again denied parole in 1994. The parole board cited the "execution style murders of four victims."

Chapter Fourteen

One Day at A Time

The shocker for Leigh was the parole board decision which denied the men another parole hearing for twenty more years. It was unprecedented.

Ohio law states that all inmates are entitled to case review every ten years. It does not state they are entitled to hearings.

Leigh did not know what was happening. "Really don't understand this move, locking me up. Others has got ten years and wasn't locked up. I'll have to lay around and listen to these big mouths back here until Monday." He wrote, "Just wanted you to know I haven't done anything wrong to be back here."

He had another surprise coming. After the weekend the warden again called Leigh into her office and told him the parole board actually had given him another twenty years, not ten. She told him he would be kept locked down in 2CB until transferred out to a different prison. That was a double dose of bad news.

"They even put me under a nut watch!" Leigh wrote. "Really, after all the bull they've put me through, I'm sure they don't believe I would hurt myself. Maybe they were thinking I may hurt someone else. Who knows? I really don't understand the transfer. Every time you get a transfer it's like starting all over again." Each prison has its own rules, he said.

"Sure wasn't looking for anything like this," John said. "If anything, they should have given me the twenty the first time I saw them, not the third time," he said. "I never heard of anyone getting twenty years at once. That's a long time. I'm going to lose a lot, Mom for sure." His mother was an elderly diabetic who was frequently hospitalized and recently was given a prognosis of about one more year of life.

"I really don't understand any of this, but I do understand that life is life. Guess I'll have to do it the best way I know how—one day at a time."

The day before his transfer John Leigh wrote, "Haven't read a paper or seen anything about my case since I saw the parole board. Guess it was really bad this time."

He was right about that. The parole board had reacted to a thunderous public outcry. The Hamilton County prosecutor held a press conference with an impassioned plea opposing parole. Relatives of three of the victims, along with friends and sympathizers, were way ahead of the prosecutor with petitions and letters asking that parole be denied. The fact that twenty-five years had passed meant nothing to those who still mourn the ugly and untimely deaths of the women who were shot down in the small bank vault.

The head of the parole board remarked, "Every time they come up for parole the board receives more mail than on any cases they ever consider."

At the time of the August 1994 hearings the board received more than seven thousand letters plus petition signatures objecting to release of the three men. Many letter writers were not initially familiar with the Cabinet Supreme story, but they or family members had been crime victims. They wrote in sympathy with the cause.

In the vanguard was Walter Rischmann, older brother of Helen Huebner. A retired lithographer, Rischmann has tracked every hearing of Leigh, Kassow and Johnson and organized letter writing campaigns about them.

In July 1994 prior to the August parole hearings Rischmann visited a parole board member in Columbus, accompanied by one of Helen's sons and two of her sisters, one of them a nun who was guidance director at a Catholic girls high school. They were told there were so many letters "they are coming in on skids."

Rischmann said, "The thing with me is having to fight this thing all the time, going through these hearings every two or five years. I kept asking him isn't there any crime that's so serious that they don't have to go through this thing?" The board member replied, "This is a thing that parole board members are kicking around right now."

The kick the board delivered was the twenty year surprise. Having broken precedent, the Ohio Parole Board did it again at a February 1995 hearing for another inmate. It extended for thirty-seven years possibility of parole for a man whose original sentence was fourteen to fifty years. He had raped, murdered and dismembered his victim. Clearly, something new is happening in Ohio's parole system.

Retrospect

From solitary, where London Warden Melody Turner put him after the hearing, Leigh wrote, "Laying around in 2CB for the past ten days, I did a lot of thinking about the past. My life on the outside was short and a mess. I've done a lot of dumb things, but nothing like this [the shootings.] Never gave life much of a thought—just trying to make it. Don't know if I would have. Maybe ending up in here was the best thing for me. But why did I have to hurt anyone?

"I keep coming back to the drinking, but I can't use that for an out. I really believe I needed someone to put a foot up my butt when I was young. I was always out on the street late at night doing dumb stuff with others, when everyone thought I was in bed. It's hard to watch all those kids all the time. It's easy to get out the window at night. Out the window when everyone was asleep, and back in before anyone got up.

"I think Mom did the best she could with what she had and knew. I needed help, but there wasn't anyone there to help me. A lot of people were there to use me up—just took a few drinks.

"There is no way I would even try to ask for forgiveness from the family. I know if I was them I wouldn't forgive. I do understand how they feel. What could I say? I'm sorry. Even that comes out cold."

Settling in at WCI

At 5:30 am on August 31, 1994, John Leigh was pulled out of his cell and taken to Warren Correctional Institution at Lebanon, Ohio, a close-maximum prison about thirty-five miles north of Cincinnati.

Unhappy about moving again, John nevertheless is pleased to be at Warren where he works as a materials handler in the commissary. For one thing, he is glad to have a prison job. Those who don't work, he says, get into fights and other trouble. He's still trying to keep his nose clean, he says.

"I just lay back and try to stay out of the way. It's the only way to do time. This [the Ohio prison system] is one hell of a school. Jailhouse 101!"

One advantage for John is that Warren Correctional is only about a half hour trip from his home town, Cincinnati. That makes it easier for some family members to visit. The visits have had an effect. John stopped shaving his head and is letting his hair grow. He no longer looks like a Hollywood stereotype, although the full beard remains.

Among those who can't visit at the time of this writing are two brothers locked up in other Ohio prisons, one on a charge of gross sexual imposition and the other for receiving stolen property. A third brother is sitting in a Cincinnati jail. John worries about them, but is more distressed about what happened to his kid brother, Billy.

Billy was only ten years old when John went to prison. The two brothers had not seen each other for twenty-five years. Billy now was a married man with a house full of children. When John was transferred to Warren, it was the first time Billy was able to visit. They spent three hours talking, a special treat for John to whom family visits are important.

Twenty-four hours later, Billy was dead in Cincinnati, shot off another brother's garage roof by an irate neighbor. The dispute, in which racial slurs were exchanged, was about kids who were throwing stones in the backyard. The sixty-two-year-old black man who shot and killed thirty-four-year-old Billy now is locked up in an Ohio prison.

"For some reason I have been having a run of bad luck with family," John notes sadly. Aside from the brothers in trouble with the law, a second uncle recently died of cancer and his mother's life expectancy is limited. These are among things that help him understand the effects of his crime.

Looking Inward

Introspection has become part of John's life. He says, "I've done a lot of things I'm not proud of when I was on the outside. One does things he may not want to do. Looking back, I know I did.

"I can't remember when I didn't run the streets. From the time I was twelve to thirteen I was on the street most of the time. Doing anything I could to make it. Running around with other kids who had even less than I did. Was always out looking for something to get into.

"Street life was hard. You never knew where or what you'd be eating next. Used to steal a lot out of cars. Kids who haven't ate for a while know how to get into a car fast when they see food on the other side of the glass.

"Always trying to make money any way you could. Some not so nice. Having sex with males and females for money at a young age. That is something I really don't like to think about, let alone talk about." He added, "Most people I knew said I would never see twenty-one. They were close, but I'm still here."

On Tattos

John describes himself at age thirteen as "settin' on a street corner with a needle and thread. Kids are still doin' it."

Most of Leigh's tattoos were acquired after 1980 in four different Ohio prisons. He says, "I sure have a lot, but there are guys here who have their whole body done. Don't think I can go that far." The "jailhouse skin" is applied with a mushfaked tattoo gun, a miscellany of scrounged items such as a bent toothbrush, a guitar string, two AA batteries and an eight-track or cassette motor. A rubber band or tape is a component, used to hold the parts together.

Tattooing "is a no-no in here. If you get caught they will put you in the hole now. Used to be, before this AIDS thing came around, they would just tell you not to do it any more. Now, it's hole time, and you have to pay for an AIDS test if they catch you."

John's tattoo designs are in demand among wanna-be illustrated men. Many of his designs feature wild looking skulls which he started drawing at Lucasville.

"I draw a lot of stuff that a biker most likely would like. And some of it is kind of crazy," he said. "I see a lot of my drawing on people in here." He says he learned how to draw tattoos by watching another inmate.

Why do men do that, especially with a woman's name? Suppose you change women?

"There's an old cartoon in the tattoo books of a sailor in a tattoo shop with a girl's name being put on his arm. And he's got a whole list on his arm. I guess the one on the bottom is the one he's going with now," John says.

What's the point of all the decorated skin?

"One thing about tattoos," says John Leigh. "They can't take them away from us."

On Getting Along

"I try, but it's hard to be nice in here. You have to come across hard most of the time. I really don't think I'm a hard person, but I do come across that way a lot in here, or when I talk to someone I don't really know. A person puts a wall around himself in here. Out there, too. I just want to be left alone. If you put on a hard face in here, troublemakers stay away from you.

"I'm easy to get along with until someone tries to hurt me or think they can say or do what they want to. I won't put up with it. I don't do it to others and I won't have it done to me. Too many things can happen in here.

"Must try to do this time one day at a time. It's the only way to do it. I've been able to understand more over the years. I can see just how messed up I was when I was young. It's sad."

Getting along and staying out of trouble isn't easy. John describes an incident which began with one inmate losing a can of tuna fish, then escalated into two brawls. Eventually, twenty-three inmates were involved. Some were punished by transfer to Lucasville.

"Last Tuesday a white guy named *Stony got some stuff took out of his cell. Wasn't much, something like a can of tuna [seventy-one cents] and a couple of soups [eighty cents] and he got his nose open. Went running his mouth that he was going to kill this nigger and that nigger—which is a no-no.

"When we went to chow that night, he didn't go and there was a fight, him and four blacks. Now no one really cares for Stony. He has a big mouth and walks around like Rambo, thinking he is better than everyone. So it was just a matter of time.

"Then on Wednesday two guys [white and black] almost got into a fight in the laundry. After they unlocked our cell doors for chow the fight started in the pod [cell block] and when two other whites got into it the fight was on.

"There was other whites there that I guess were Aryan Brothers and so-called friends of the three, but no one even tried to help them.

"The three whites are always talking about the blacks and putting them down, and they run with the Aryan Brothers here which isn't about anything—just a lot of young fools that really don't understand what real jail is like.

"The guards locked us in our cells for the rest of the day. Guards went from cell to cell, checking our hands to see if they were red, and anyone who looked like their hands had been in a fight went to the hole. I almost went because of my tattoos, being I have a lot of white trash tattoos on me.

"I was asked did I belong to the Aryan Brothers or any other gang. I said no. Which I don't. They asked me if my tattoos caused me any trouble with the blacks in here. I said no, which they don't. I get along good with the blacks. I know so many of them from other places, a lot from Lucasville. They know I don't play that AB stuff. I will walk away from a fight if I can. I used not to be able to do that.

"The night before most of the guys who were in the fight were drunk on homemade wine." Leigh said some were sent to Lucasville and some were sent to nearby Lebanon prison.

"Anyway, things are back the way they were. Everyone has forgot about it, which is dumb, because it could happen again at any time. Just glad I don't get into that kind of stuff any more. Never did, really.

"Most of the fights I got into was one on one. There is always a time to fight and a place. A lot of times it is just head games, a guy running his mouth because his friends are around. There is a time to walk away. You see the guy later without his friends, and he's just the nicest guy here. Got to know when to fight. A person's mouth can get him killed real fast in these places."

Leigh has one advantage in getting along. Other inmates, he says, "don't really like to mess with oldtimers like me. Too many jailhouse associates. You don't have to be an asshole or a bully to make it in here. You do have to use your head and not your mouth."

Inside Interests

In-house wine making is a popular pastime. In December John wrote, "Shook us all down today, looking for wine. Didn't find any. Everyone was already drunk." In just about every prison where John has been, surreptitious moonshiners are busy creating the innovative potable. The homemade product "makes fools want to fight, like the last time," John says. He comments, "Don't see what they get out of that stuff in here. Get low, feel like buffalo chips and get sick—and they pay for this. Must be crazy." The reformed drinker thinks like Mark Twain's *Pudd'nhead Wilson*: "Nothing so needs reforming as other people's habits."

There are other things inmates can do. Ohio prisons have softball diamonds, gyms and running tracks. Some have additional facilities. John sticks to his paint brushes because athletic areas are often used to release aggressions. Even a casual walk around a running track can put you in the path of some who have a great need to push and pummel. Still, letting out frustration that way is better than free-for-alls and worse in the cell block, he indicates.

The system-wise inmate says, "Life is hell in here, but we make do with what we have. Some of us are better at it than others. Some of us know that a brick wall is better than a mud wall. So we know how to stay out of trouble better. You learn how to read people in here."

On Other Inmates

John sidesteps questions about what other inmates are in for. He doesn't ask, he says. "He might be in on a child molesting charge and I might not like that. What I don't know don't bother me."

It's said that men who are in on child molesting don't fare too well in prison. Is that true?

"Years ago it used to be like that. Now it seems like everybody accepts it because it seems like half the guys who come in here has got charges like that. When I came in, it might have been one or two, but now if they bring thirty guys in, at least ten of them are here on some kind of sex charge."

While inmate policy may be "don't ask" it does not include "don't tell" and today's young offenders are not reticent. They talk about anything and everything.

John says, "You wouldn't believe it. They got guys in here for writing checks on their mom and dad, and mom and dad won't press charges, but the state picks them up and locks them up. And while they're in here, they get turned out, they make homosexuals out of them. It's bad news."

Isn't there a way for the administration to control that?

"The administration don't care. They turn their backs until you get caught in the act, and that's when they throw you in the hole.

"I'd say ninety percent of these guys here right now are in on drug-related charges. Most of them are young. Most of them belong to little street gangs. These guys nowadays are mostly jive. They're not what you'd call real criminals, bank robbers and stuff like that. A lot of these guys don't even belong in here, but they need a good butt-kicking. A lot them, this place ain't gonna help them none at all."

Maybe, but what are you going to do with them?

"Yeah. I'm glad it ain't my choice."

The prison view of the generation gap does not differ greatly from the view outside the bars. Young people don't follow rules and are hard to deal with. "It's harder to put up with the type of people that are coming in here now," John says. They get used to liking it in here; that's why they keep coming back.

"They can belong to a lot of things in here that they couldn't do on the outside—baseball teams; no bills to pay; workout with weights when they don't have to be at work; hang out with their so-called friends who really don't want to do anything but get them into trouble.

"They should think about all the things they had on the outside—little things that no one really thinks about, like eating when you want to, eating food you like when you may want it; taking a shower without ten other guys with you; going to the movies; walking in the rain; not wearing blues every day of the year; not having to listen to a radio with headphones all the time. A person can miss a lot.

"I think at times what I have missed, like all of the '70s and '80s, and most likely all of the '90's. I still hope to get out of here someday. I just hope it's before I'm too old to do anything for myself."

Chapter Fifteen

Life After Murder

When her mother was murdered Rosemary Stitzel, a bookkeeper for eleven years, was vacationing in Fort Lauderdale, Florida. She came home to shock and horror. She testified during the trials and eventually was able to put the terrible event behind her.

Twenty-five years later, Rosemary and her sisters still talk fondly of tea and toast and other good times with Aunt Luella. As a girl, Rosemary said, she considered her mother to be quite old, but comforted herself with the thought that if her mother died, there would always be the younger Aunt Luella to turn to.

They had lost their father and a brother. Then, with their mother and aunt both dead at once, "We felt like the rug had been pulled out from under us."

They still had Uncle Nick, retired from his job at a Cincinnati dairy foods firm, aged and using a cane, but a comforting presence. "He was always there to welcome us home from school or work."

When Nick died in 1978 at age seventy-nine, the sisters who were still at home no longer felt comfortable without Nick in the old Denver Street house, especially since the neighborhood was changing. A year later they sold the house for a nominal sum. Rosemary and her sister, Marilyn, now share a home in a different part of town.

* * *

138

Walter Dewald became a Cincinnati police officer in 1950 after serving in the merchant marine and working in a bakery. He enjoyed fishing and baseball, and also picked up some cash as a professional dance instructor. He and Lillian Feist, married in 1953, both liked to go bowling and were members of a Delhi team. When Lillian was killed on September 24, 1969 Walter was a patrolman in the Traffic Bureau, working radar on the interstate. Contacted on police radio, Dewald drove to Cabinet Supreme in Delhi, but other officers on the scene would not allow him to go inside and see his murdered wife, lying in a pool of blood.

Dewald's friends believe his trip to Canada the week before the holdup was a long deferred fishing trip with like-minded police buddies. He probably felt it was safe to go fishing because the savings and loan manager had returned from vacation and Lillian was no longer alone in the office.

Before the trials were over, Dewald sold the house he had shared with Lillian. He remarried in 1971 and was promoted to police specialist in 1973. After twenty-nine years of service with the department Dewald retired in 1979 and now lives in Florida.

*　　*　　*

Joe Huebner also remarried. He lives with his second wife in the same Delhi home where he and Helen raised their three sons, Tom, Larry and Danny. All three now are married men, fathers of five boys and a girl, grandchildren Helen never had a chance to see.

Walter Rischmann never forgot holding the telephone and hearing his nephew, Tom Huebner, screaming when the young sailor was told his mother had been shot to death.

Rischmann followed the trials and thought the matter was brought to closure after the three men responsible were sentenced to death. When their sentences were commuted to life imprisonment, he started to keep track.

When parole hearings were held in 1984 and again in 1989, Walter Rischmann was ready with letters and signed petitions protesting parole.

He knew hearings again would be held sometime in the middle of 1994, so in March he called the parole board office in the state capital to learn the date. What he learned was that Leigh and Johnson had filed applications for a work-release program, and a hearing on the request was scheduled for April.

Work-release puts former prisoners in a communal residence, usually in the area where they were living when they went to prison. While they must sleep in a supervised residence, during daylight hours these persons are expected to go out, unsupervised, and look for jobs.

Walter acted. He circulated petitions objecting to "any work schedule furlough or early parole," citing the "premeditated, horrible, senseless slaughter" of the four women. He was methodical. He left copies of the petitions at the town hall and other public places. He left them at the Delhi Senior Citizens meeting place, taking care to include self-addressed, stamped envelopes. "These are the people who really remember," Rischmann says.

In early April, he and one of his sisters were in Columbus for a lengthy meeting with two members of the parole board, presenting 1,300 signatures and three hundred additional letters protesting the work-release proposal.

That was effective. Work-release was denied. After the hearings, which were accompanied by considerable publicity, Rischmann wrote thank you letters to newspapers and television stations.

Because Rischmann learned that parole hearings were scheduled for August of the same year, he knew he could not cease his efforts. Buoyed by newspaper reports and televised protests to parole from the county prosecutor, Rischmann redoubled his efforts, resulting in "tons of mail" sent to the parole board.

"The letters came from Delhi, Westwood, Cheviot and Bridgetown and all the surrounding neighborhoods of the Western Hills area of Cincinnati," said Walter. "Some came from Cincinnati and some from way back in Kentucky. Friends and relatives were taking them [the petitions] into hospitals and plants where they work and other places for people to sign these things." Following publicity, Rischmann received letters from people he never heard of, but who felt victimized.

"One had a niece, another had a brother, one had a father—I mean they all had problems."

Rischmann was told the most the board could do was to set back parole possibility for ten years. When he later was told that the new parole board ruling meant the men in prison would not be eligible for parole again for twenty years he was "surprised and elated."

The retired lithographer returned to his routine, helping his wife, Ruth, babysit their great-grandkids and playing golf every Wednesday. Shortly afterwards, Walter collapsed on the golf course. He had no previous history of heart ailment, but he wound up with multiple bypass surgery in a Cincinnati hospital. A determined man, Walter Rischmann is recovering well, Ruth says. He has lost some weight, the hard way, and is ready to play golf again.

The next scheduled parole hearing date for Leigh, Kassow and Johnson is 2014. The youngest, Leigh will be sixty-five years old. Walter Rischmann will be ninety-four. If he is not around, Walter says, the next generation will pick up the task.

"Oh, yes," says Danny Huebner, a thirty-eight-year-old man who at age thirteen was pulled out of his classroom to be told his mother had been murdered. "Me and my brother and my Rischmann cousins, too."

*   *   *

John Leigh's mother, Ruby, was plagued for many years by heart problems and diabetes. Eventually she lost some toes to the diabetes. Then in December 1995, a leg was amputated. Confined to a nursing home the last few months of her life, she succumbed on April 8, 1996 at the age of sixty-six.

Ruby Burton Mitchell, mother of fourteen children with four different last names, was buried at Cincinnati's historic Spring Grove Cemetery. Nearby lie John's grandmother, Rachel Burton, who helped raise him; his Uncle "Boots" Vernon Burton, who taught him the hazards of bar fights, and Ruby's tenth child, the only one to pre-decease her. That was Billy Mitchell who at age thirty-four was shot dead off a garage roof by an irate neighbor.

"Mom and I were going to have a picture taken together when she visited me on April 14," said John. He knew his mother's hold on life was precarious, but had hoped for just a little more time with her and for the picture as a keepsake.

While John was permitted, under restraints, to attend the funeral of his grandmother in the 1970s when he was at the Lucasville prison, he was not permitted to go to his mother's funeral in 1996 because, he said, he was told he is "too high profile."

*   *   *

Rita Leigh and Betty Kassow, Ray's wife, both obtained divorces. Betty's maiden name was restored by the courts. Rita is reported to have left the state.

*   *   *

Four of the Delhi Township officers involved at the outset of the crime, including the chief, still are on the job.

Five large case books containing verbatim crime investigation reports, background data and related photographs covered the holdup-murders in painstaking detail from July 12, when Kassow and Johnson first came to the attention of Delhi police, to grand jury indictments on October 13, 1969.

The collection of information was meticulously assembled and periodically summarized and annotated by Chief Makin. A wrap-up summary of sixty-five pages in testimony for the grand jury built a case so strong that investigators and prosecutors believed convictions were inevitable even if there had been no confessions.

Dr. Frank Cleveland, recently retired after three decades as Hamilton County coroner, used those case books for years as exemplars in how to prepare a case for the prosecutor, in seminars which drew officers from all over the United States and Canada.

Cooperation among area police departments and coordinated mutual aid marked the manhunt which got underway within minutes after the four women met death in Delhi. Chief Makin called for help and expressed appreciation for the "three hundred or so" police officers active in the investigation.

Agencies involved eventually included the Delhi Police Department; Cincinnati Police; the Hamilton County Sheriff's Department; the FBI; New Mexico State Police; the Bureau of Criminal Investigation in London, Ohio; the county coroner's office and the Alcohol, Tobacco and Firearms laboratory in Washington, D.C. It was a massive effort.

As the man at the helm, Makin was lauded for his leadership and thoroughness. The speed with which verdicts were reached was attributed by two of the trial judges "to the thorough groundwork of the Delhi Police Department."

Judge William J. Morrissey noted that much work was done prior to the crime. He praised what he described as "an outstanding piece of police work."

Judge William S. Mathews commended Makin "for sound judgment and professionalism in handling the case."

Makin now has been a working cop for thirty-four years, police chief for thirty-two of them. In June 1994 at the state attorney general's conference he was presented with a special service award which cited his active involvement and leadership in CLEAR (County Law Enforcement Applied Regionally) which was responsible for the first regional automated fingerprint system in Ohio, and the Mobile Data Terminal System which links more than five hundred police vehicles directly to dispatch systems.

*   *   *

Bob Chetwood was in his first year with the Delhi department when the four women were murdered, but he was not a novice. He had spent one-and-a-half years with the Cincinnati Police Department where his father was a seasoned officer, then decided that was not for him. He went to work in a bank, but missed the adrenalin rush that comes with emergency response.

He became a volunteer fireman and qualified as an emergency medical technician with the life squad. Nine years after starting as a Cincinnati officer, Chetwood went back into police work, this time with the Delhi department. He gave up banking, but not the life squad.

The day of the holdup was Chetwood's day off from the cop shop, but he was with the life squad crew which answered the call to Cabinet Supreme. It was an odd mixture of responsibilities. As it happened, there was no one left alive to take to the hospital, so he automatically responded to police obligations. Five years later, Chetwood relinquished his avocation with the volunteer fire department to which he had given eleven years.

Bob Chetwood's first year with Delhi was his father's last year with Cincinnati Police. The two Chetwoods were policemen at the same time for about ten months. The elder Chetwood retired after twenty-six years, but the younger Chetwood, now in his twenty-seventh year of police work, does not talk of retirement. Promoted to lieutenant, Bob is in charge of all criminal investigations for the Delhi department. He never forgets what he learned during the Cabinet Supreme investigation.

"The cooperation and assistance from Cincinnati never wavered," he says. "Those guys worked fourteen to sixteen hours a day and never complained." He watched expert interrogator Frank Sefton, Cincinnati police detective, as he questioned suspects.

"I was young and impatient and wanted to yell at these guys to tell me the truth. Frank would take me aside and explain that doesn't get results." Sefton had a reputation for developing rapport with suspects. He would lull them into conversation. They told him things. Chetwood says he learned, "Treat 'em nice and you get more."

* * *

Don Jasper had just gone off duty, but was in the chief's office when the radio in the police station came alive with report of the holdup that day in 1969. Like Makin, he has been with the department from its early days. Their good working relationship has endured during the more than thirty years they have served Delhi together.

Lieutenant Jasper's responsibilities now are mostly administrative, but once in a while he gets back into the field. There is a difference, he says. He tells about a brouhaha brewing on a ballfield with a bunch of angry teenagers. He waded into the middle of it, and in his familiar bull-horn voice, told them to break it up. That worked, he said, but later he asked himself, "What in hell am I doing? I was alone and today's teenagers are not like yesterday's." Anyone of them could have been carrying a weapon.

Jasper's confidence with youngsters comes from twenty-six years in scout work. He especially enjoys working with Cub Scouts, he says, under the theory that the younger you teach them the right stuff, the more likely the lesson will last.

* * *

Lt. John Eschenbach, a four year veteran of the U.S. Marine Corps and a Delhi police officer for thirty years, now is in command of the department's road patrol. This is the officer who responded to a defense attorney's off-beat question at Leigh's trial with the acerbic "It was not a routine call for our department, sir." He talks about how it was when the department was faced with the horrible crime in their community.

"We learned that you never know what you may be faced with. Men who were on-duty, off-duty, all worked as a unit. Time doesn't mean anything. You do what you have to do." He was impressed not only with how the men in the department pulled together, but with the" tremendous outpouring of community support." People volunteered time and effort, supplied coffee, food, and did whatever they could do to assist those who were putting everything they had into the manhunt. The department still is grateful for community support. "You couldn't replace the experience you get from these things," Eschenbach says.

Experience and stress took their toll. In January 1995, John suffered triple aneurysms. Surgery and physical therapy have put Lieutenant Eschenbach back on his feet. Those who know him well know that dogged determination had a great deal to do with recovery.

Networking

The value of interagency police communication and cooperation was brought home to Delhi during the investigation of the Cabinet Supreme holdup-murders.

The National Crime Information Center, known across the country as NCIC, was responsible for the capture of John Leigh and Watterson Johnson four days after they fled Cincinnati.

NCIC became operational in 1967, with fifteen cooperating agencies. By the end of the first year the computerized filing system had logged 2.5 million transactions. By the end of 1991 there were 70,000 police agencies involved, logging 402 million items, an average of one million per day. By definition, those items are "information collected by criminal justice agencies that is needed for performance of their legally authorized and required functions."

Sometimes that definition is bent by an officer in learning mode. A patrolman in a small suburb north of Cincinnati once created a stir when he teletyped a query on Patricia Hearst, the newspaper magnate's daughter who was kidnapped, then sought by the Federal Bureau of Investigation. NCIC instantly responded with a total description. Inquiries poured in to the little suburban department from throughout the county. Said the officer's chief, "It's a good thing the FBI didn't pick up on the query because he was just practicing his homework in a course on how to use communications equipment."

Operated by the FBI, NCIC functions twenty-four hours a day, seven days a week. The agency says about "ninety-nine percent of usage is by state, local and other federal agencies." The system provides access to criminal history records which are stored by category: stolen vehicles and license plates; stolen and recovered guns; stolen securities and other items; missing persons; foreign fugitives and violent felons, among many other things.

As with other computers, the GIGO factor applies: garbage-in, garbage-out. What you get out of it is only as good as what you put in. NCIC is dependent for accuracy on the multitude of police agencies which submit data for transmission. When New Mexico state troopers picked up the Cabinet Supreme fugitives, they got a "hit" on John Leigh, but not on Watterson Johnson, initially. That was because the local operator had transmitted his name as Johnson Watterson. When the error was corrected, the second hit came in.

Hamilton County's Regional Computer Information Center (RCIC) was connected with the national center March 1969, two years after NCIC inception. The RCIC first formal message announced "service will initialize full operations at 1030 March 20, 1969." It proved of value in the Cabinet Supreme case in September.

Heading into the next century, by the fall of 1999 NCIC will be calling itself NCIC 2000 to reflect augmented capabilities, some of which are already in place. The improved system will include the addition of image processing such as mug shots, signature and identifying marks; automated single-finger fingerprint matching; access to new databases such as lists of convicted persons on parole, and the Canadian Police Information Center (CPIC). NCIC 2000 also will have the ability to associate multiple records with the same criminal or the same crime, and automatic collection of statistics for system evaluation.

Of particular interest to communities which see growth of gang activities will be use of an Illinois State Police program called VITAL—Violent Crime Tracking and Linking system which provides photographic images of known gang members.

The FBI, which operates the national crime computer system, cautions that "Implementation of NCIC 2000 will require each state to update its law enforcement network." It will be a major expense for each state which wants to make full use of the system.

Addendum

A spate of retirements has changed the picture at the Delhi Police Department since this book was written. Three of the four officers involved in the Cabinet Supreme investigation hung it up in February, April and May of 1996.

Lt. Bob Chetwood surprised his peers when he closed out twenty-eight years of service with the Delhi department on February 28. Learning of the impending retirement of the man who had been his boss and his guide through almost three decades, Chetwood decided it was time for him, too, to leave.

Lt. John Eschenbach called it quits on April 30 after thirty-one years in the system, still valiantly and successfully battling effects of triple aneurysms.

And Chief Howard Makin ended his thirty-five year career with a May 28 retirement.

The departure of Makin sparked interest throughout Hamilton County police circles where he is fondly known as "The Godfather." That nickname derives not just from Makin's longevity on the job as the only chief the Delhi department ever had, but also because of the many law enforcement officers who call him "mentor." The man's steady pace towards continuing improvements not only defined the growing township police department; his influence has been felt in the entire area.

Party planners decided that the only fitting place for "The Godfather's" retirement party was a banquet facility called "The Syndicate" (in Newport, Kentucky). Guests who arrived dressed as flappers and "wise guys" livened the evening and augmented the decor which included antique cars and a guard with a "tommy" gun. The Thompson machine gun was real, although it had been plugged for safety. Former owner of the gun was the grandmother of one of Delhi's officers, a woman who owned a saloon in a different era.

147

Attended by almost four hundred people, the affair lasted more than five hours because of numerous agencies and persons eager to make presentations to the retiree. That included the Federal Bureau of Investigation, the Secret Service, the Bureau of Alcohol, Tobacco and Firearms, the Regional Computer Information Center, area police and police chiefs associations and most area police departments.

One mark of the stability of the Delhi Police Department is that retirement of the police chief and two lieutenants did not produce the usual feeding frenzy of job applicants from other police agencies. All of those positions have been filled by promotion from within the ranks.

Additum

John Leigh once told this writer, "Most people I knew said I would never see twenty-one. They were close, but I'm still here." Not any more.

He also said he hoped to get out of prison before he was too old to do anything for himself. Doesn't matter now. He is dead.

John Levi Leigh died in a prison hospital at the age of 51. Incarcerated at Warren Correctional Institution near Lebanon, Ohio, he was transferred to the state prison at Orient, Ohio on October 20, 2000, then to the Corrections Medical Facility in Columbus where he died on November 14. Official cause of death was listed as liver disease.

The spokesman for the Department of Corrections was asked, "How does a man who has been on a state diet for about 30 years develop liver disease?"

He laughed and said, "I have no idea."

The Cabinet Supreme Savings & Loan, Delhi Township, as it looked on September 24, 1969.

John Leigh, age 20, also known as Johnny France, as he looked when arrested by Cincinnati Police in 1968.

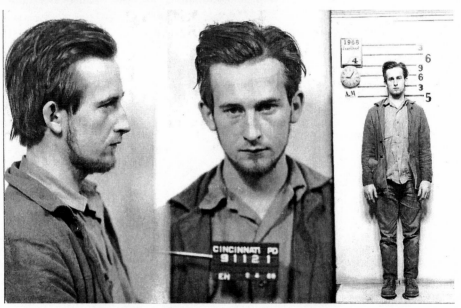

NAME (Print — Last Name First)
KASSOW RAYMOND

LOCATION: *Greenwell & Foley*

DATE INTERROGATED: 8-3 19 69   TIME 4:30 AM

BEAT NO. 829C   CENSUS TRACT NO.

SUBJECT'S ADDRESS: 1326 Denver   BIRTH DATE 24 19   SEX M

RACE	HEIGHT	WEIGHT	HAIR	EYES	COMPL	MARKS · SCARS · DEFORMITIES
W	6'0"	220	BK		DK	

DESCRIPTION OF CLOTHING

VEHICLE (YEAR - MAKE - BODY) 67 Falcon 2 DR GRW Green or Blue   COLOR(S) DK   LICENSE (YEAR - STATE - NO.) 69 OL 85359?

OPERATOR'S LICENSE (STATE - NO. - TYPE) (Two lightning strips on rear)

DELHI TWP. POLICE DISTRICT
934 NEEB ROAD **FIELD INTERROGATION REPORT**
Cincinnati Police Form 534 435238   (See Other Side)

COMPANIONS (Make Separate Card on Each):
Johnson Watterson
SUBJECT'S EMPLOYER & BUSINESS ADDRESS   (IF JUVENILE, NAME SCHOOL)

REASON FOR INTERROGATION
Driver of car loaded with clothing on rear seat. Stated they were looking for Goodwill Box, however they passed up 2

REPORTING OFFICER(S): Eschenbach - Mondary

SUBJECT'S I. S. NO.   PRIOR RECORD   MISD. (X)   FELONY (X) ✓   SUBSEQUENT DEVELOPMENTS

Picture obtained and placed on Bull. Bd. See report on Tropical Foliage

---

The Field Interrogation Report cards on Ray Kassow and Watterson Johnson, completed by Delhi Police Officer Eschenbach and Cincinnati Police Officer Bob Mondary, six weeks before the murders. Note the cross-referencing of the two cards. Also, note the reference to the Tropical Foliage store, where Kassow and Johnson had been earlier in the week.

NAME (Print — Last Name First)
JOHNSON WATTERSON

LOCATION: *Greenwell & Foley*

DATE INTERROGATED: 8-3 19 69   TIME 4:30 AM

BEAT NO. 829-C   CENSUS TRACT NO.

SUBJECT'S ADDRESS: 1706 Race St.   BIRTH DATE 9-8 1948 19   SEX M

RACE	HEIGHT	WEIGHT	HAIR	EYES	COMPL	MARKS · SCARS · DEFORMITIES
W	6'2"	210	Red	Blu	Lt	

DESCRIPTION OF CLOTHING

VEHICLE (YEAR - MAKE - BODY)   COLOR(S) Curly   LICENSE (YEAR - STATE - NO.)

OPERATOR'S LICENSE (STATE - NO. - TYPE)

DELHI TWP. POLICE DISTRICT
934 NEEB ROAD **FIELD INTERROGATION REPORT**
Cincinnati Police Form 534 435238   (See Other Side)

COMPANIONS (Make Separate Card on Each):
Kassow Raymond
SUBJECT'S EMPLOYER & BUSINESS ADDRESS   (IF JUVENILE, NAME SCHOOL)

REASON FOR INTERROGATION
Was passenger in car driven by companion. Kassow. Car loaded with clothing on rear seat. Stated they were looking for a Goodwill Box

REPORTING OFFICER(S): Eschenbach - Mondary

SUBJECT'S I. S. NO.   PRIOR RECORD   MISD. (X)   FELONY (X) ✓   SUBSEQUENT DEVELOPMENTS

No Picture Available. See Report on Tropical Foliage

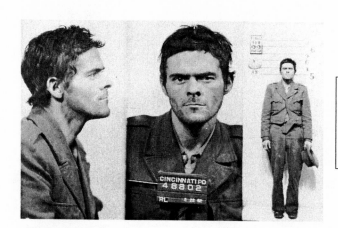

LEFT: Richard Vernon Burton, Leigh's "Uncle Boots" in a 1962 arrest photo.

RIGHT: The car Leigh borrowed to use in the robbery.

Entrance to the crime scene protected by a Delhi police officer.

Cabinet Supreme's parking lot right after the crime. The car in the left foreground is the Huebner's. The white Chevrolet at upper right, facing the building, belonged to the Stitzels. The two-toned car next to it was Lillian Dewald's.

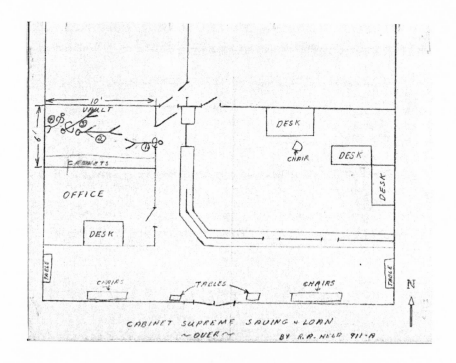

A sketch of the crime scene done by a detective at the time of the investigation. The vault, with stick figures representing the victims, is at left.

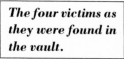

The four victims as they were found in the vault.

ABOVE: Raymond Kassow, age 24, in custody hours after the murders.

LEFT: Hamilton County Police Lieutenant Herb Vogel interviewing Kassow

BELOW: The guns used in the murders. The .25 automatic, at right, fired five times, then jammed; .22 revolver, left, fired twice then jammed; .22 revolver in center was kept in the car.

LEFT: Watterson "Red" Johnson in custody in New Mexico

BELOW: Watterson Johnson, age 22, in custody in Hamilton County after being returned from New Mexico.

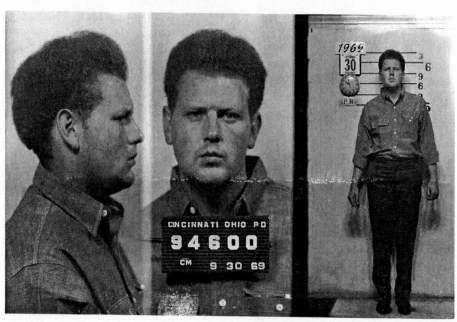

RIGHT: *John Levi Leigh, in custody in New Mexico.*

BELOW: *John Leigh, in custody in Hamilton County after being returned from New Mexico*

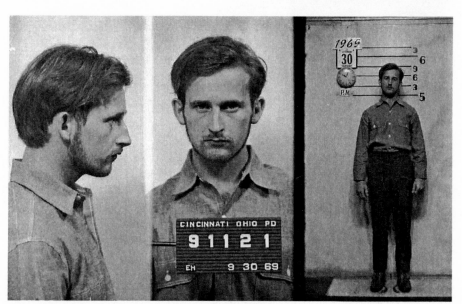

157

ABOVE: The witnesses view Leigh and Johnson in a line up.

BELOW: The line up. Leigh is holding #4, Johnson #5.

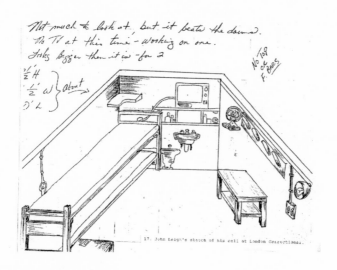

Not much to look at, but it beats the dorms. No TV at this time - working on one. Looks bigger then it is - for 2

½ H ½ W } about 9' L

17. John Leigh's sketch of his cell at London Correctional.

ABOVE: Leigh's sketch of his cell at London Correctional Facility.

RIGHT: Leigh shows how to hide money in prison.

BELOW: Lucasville prison as Leigh depicted it. Note the signature "Ice" and year, center right. SOCF on cap identifies the Southern Ohio Correctional Facility.

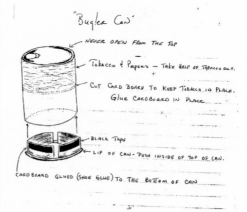

"Bugler Can"

- NEVER OPEN FROM THE TOP
- TOBACCO & PAPERS — TAKE HALF OF TOBACCO OUT.
- CUT CARDBOARD TO KEEP TOBACCO IN PLACE. GLUE CARDBOARD IN PLACE.
- BLACK TAPE
- LIP OF CAN - PUSH INSIDE OF TOP OF CAN.
- CARDBOARD GLUED (SHOE GLUE) TO THE BOTTOM OF CAN

LEFT: John Leigh, age 45, in prison

BELOW: Delhi Police Chief Howard Makin, reviewing the five case books on the crime, 1969.

LEFT: Delhi Police Chief Howard Makin, honored at an awards ceremony in Columbus, Ohio, 1994

BELOW: The Huebners. From left, Tommy at age 18; his murdered mother, Helen; his father, Joe, who found the victims. (photo courtesy Tom Huebner.)

About the Author

"Kate, you better get back here quick. There's been a holdup in Delhi. Four women have been shot." It was the office of the Price Hills News calling Kate March. She had been its editor for just a year and a half.

She would win an award from the Ohio Newspaper Association for her coverage of the tale of "The Cabinet Supreme Murders."

Kate March worked 18 years as a newspaper woman, mostly editing weekly newspapers in suburban Cincinnati and in Lombard, Illinois. She was a stringer for the *Cincinnati Enquirer* and was on the staff of the Pulitzer Prize winning *Daily Gazette* of Xenia, Ohio. She has received numerous awards for her tight writing and clear prose.

She has covered crime stories and police departments large and small and was exposed to such strangeness as being called as a juror in a sensational murder case about which she had written the original news stories.

The most gripping of all her stories, she says, is the Cabinet Supreme murders, which is told in this book, from the dissolute and corrupt youth of the shooter plus his violent and illicit activities as a convict, through the time he became an acquiescent inmate.

Kate March died February 6, 2007, in her 80th year of life.

Index